INVITATION TO MARK

INVITATION TO MARK

*A Commentary on the Gospel of Mark with
Complete Text from The Jerusalem Bible*

PAUL J. ACHTEMEIER

IMAGE BOOKS
A Division of Doubleday & Company, Inc.
Garden City, New York

The text of the Gospel According to Mark is from The Jerusalem Bible, Copyright © 1966 by Darton, Longman & Todd, Ltd., and Doubleday & Company, Inc. Used by permission of the publisher.

ISBN: 0-385-12213-6
Library of Congress Catalog Card Number: 77-91555
Commentary Copyright © 1978 by Paul J. Achtemeier
General Introduction Copyright © 1977 by Robert J. Karris

For Marie—
she knows why

CONTENTS

ABBREVIATIONS OF THE BOOKS OF THE BIBLE

Ac	Acts	Lk	Luke
Am	Amos	Lm	Lamentations
Ba	Baruch	Lv	Leviticus
1 Ch	1 Chronicles	1 M	1 Maccabees
2 Ch	2 Chronicles	2 M	2 Maccabees
1 Co	1 Corinthians	Mi	Micah
2 Co	2 Corinthians	Mk	Mark
Col	Colossians	Ml	Malachi
Dn	Daniel	Mt	Matthew
Dt	Deuteronomy	Na	Nahum
Ep	Ephesians	Nb	Numbers
Est	Esther	Ne	Nehemiah
Ex	Exodus	Ob	Obadiah
Ezk	Ezekiel	1 P	1 Peter
Ezr	Ezra	2 P	2 Peter
Ga	Galatians	Ph	Philippians
Gn	Genesis	Phm	Philemon
Hab	Habakkuk	Pr	Proverbs
Heb	Hebrews	Ps	Psalms
Hg	Haggai	Qo	Ecclesiastes
Ho	Hosea	Rm	Romans
Is	Isaiah	Rt	Ruth
Jb	Job	Rv	Revelation
Jdt	Judith	1 S	1 Samuel
Jg	Judges	2 S	2 Samuel
Jl	Joel	Sg	Song of Songs
Jm	James	Si	Ecclesiasticus
Jn	John	Tb	Tobit
1 Jn	1 John	1 Th	1 Thessalonians
2 Jn	2 John	2 Th	2 Thessalonians
3 Jn	3 John	1 Tm	1 Timothy
Jon	Jonah	2 Tm	2 Timothy
Jos	Joshua	Tt	Titus
Jr	Jeremiah	Ws	Wisdom
Jude	Jude	Zc	Zechariah
1 K	1 Kings	Zp	Zephaniah
2 K	2 Kings		

GENERAL INTRODUCTION TO THE DOUBLEDAY NEW TESTAMENT COMMENTARY SERIES

Let me introduce this new commentary series on the New Testament by sharing some experiences. In my job as New Testament Book Review Editor for the *Catholic Biblical Quarterly,* scores of books pass through my hands each year. As I evaluate these books and send them out to reviewers, I cannot help but think that so little of this scholarly research will make its way into the hands of the educated lay person.

In talking at biblical institutes and to charismatic and lay study groups, I find an almost unquenchable thirst for the Word of God. People want to learn more; they want to study. But when they ask me to recommend commentaries on the New Testament, I'm stumped. What commentaries can I put into their hands, commentaries that do not have the technical jargon of scholars and that really communicate to the educated laity?

The goal of this popular commentary series is to make the best of contemporary scholarship available to

the educated lay person in a highly readable and understandable way. The commentaries avoid footnotes and
other scholarly apparatus. They are short and sweet.
The authors make their points in a clear way and don't
fatigue their readers with unnecessary detail.

Another outstanding feature of this commentary
series is that it is based on The Jerusalem Bible translation, which is serialized with the commentary. This
lively and easily understandable translation has received rave reviews from millions of readers. It is the
interstate of translations and avoids the stoplights of
local-road translations.

A signal feature of the commentaries on the Gospels
is that they explore the way each evangelist used the
sayings and deeds of Jesus to meet the needs of his
church. The commentators answer the question: How
did each evangelist guide, challenge, teach, and console
the members of his community with the message of
Jesus? The commentators are not interested in the
evangelist's message for its own sake, but explain that
message with one eye on present application.

This last-mentioned feature goes hand and glove
with the innovative feature of appending Study Questions to the explanations of individual passages. By
means of these Study Questions the commentator
moves from an explanation of the message of the evangelist to a consideration of how this message might
apply to believers today.

Each commentator has two highly important qualifications: scholarly expertise and the proven ability
to communicate the results of solid scholarship to the
people of God.

I am confident that this new commentary series will

meet a real need as it helps people to unlock a door to the storehouse of God's Word, where they will find food for life.

ROBERT J. KARRIS, O.F.M.
Associate Professor of New Testament Studies,
Catholic Theological Union and
Chicago Cluster of Theological Schools

INTRODUCTION

As in any book of this kind, my debt to fellow Scripture scholars must remain unacknowledged in detail. One of the happier facts of our age is the manner in which the study of the Bible has transcended all national and confessional boundaries. In many ways, so far as the study of Scripture is concerned, the ecumenical problem has been solved. And I here happily acknowledge that I have profited greatly from that fact.

This commentary is characterized as much by what I have not said as by what I have found room to say. I have left much unsaid, partly for reasons of space, partly because I do not feel reliable answers have as yet been uncovered. Much work has been done in this earliest of the Gospels, but much remains to be done. Perhaps those who read these pages will catch something of the excitement of a journey of discovery well begun, but still far from ended. God has yet more truth to bring forth from his Word.

These pages are intended to be read in the context of the faith of Christ's church. When they are, they will be read within the context and intention of that early Christian who wrote the gospel pages upon which this commentary is based.

PROBLEMS MARK HAD TO SOLVE

Before the author of our Gospel of Mark set out to write an account of the career of Jesus, nothing comparable to it had existed. According to the impression we get from the first chapters of Acts, the church, despite some opposition, was growing and thriving. Why would someone go to all the trouble of composing a Gospel if the church was doing well without it? Yet there are hints, both in Acts and in the Gospel of Mark, that in fact things were not going all that smoothly. Perhaps we can discover, from such hints, what some of the problems were that moved the author of Mark to invent a whole new kind of literature in order to solve them. From certain emphases present in Mark's Gospel we can discern at least three problems: the problem of the destruction of the Temple and Jesus' second coming (especially in chapter 13); the problem involved in following a crucified Lord; and the problem involved in understanding the importance of the cross for the meaning of the career of Jesus. If we examine those problems, we will be in a better position to understand some of the things the author of Mark was trying to do when he (or she!—we really don't know anything about the author, except from some later guesses) set out to write an account of the career of Jesus.

THE DESTRUCTION OF THE TEMPLE

First, then, the destruction of the Temple. Palestine had never taken kindly to its Roman occupation, and ever since Herod the Great forced himself on the Jews as their king in 37 B.C. (with Rome's permission and encouragement, of course), they had been looking for a way to drive out those hated enemies. The revolt that had long been brewing broke out in A.D. 66, and after mopping up in Galilee, the Romans laid siege to Jerusalem. Once and for all, they intended to put down this rebellious people who had for so long given them so much trouble. The siege ended in 70, with the capture of Jerusalem and the burning of a large part of the city, including the Temple. As in all such cases, looting and murder, pillage and rape accompanied the occupying troops. But was the fall of Jerusalem and the destruction of the Temple just an outgrowth of Roman military policy, or was it God's way of punishing the Jews for their continuing rejection of Jesus? Such a question could not have been far from the minds of the Christians who lived during those events. If the center of Jewish worship had been destroyed, could that not mean that God was now prepared to bring history to a close by sending his Son to complete the judgment of all humanity? Could this not be the first in that final series of events that would announce the end of the kingdoms of this world and the coming of God's own kingdom? Then, as now, there were people who thought they found evidence that Jesus would return very soon. Yet if Christians came to believe that, what excesses of belief and action that could touch off! What incalculable harm such a false notion could mean for the church! Somehow, this event needed to be set in proper perspective, so that Christians would not take the kind of action that was appropriate only for the time when Jesus actually did return with power as judge of all the earth.

THREATENING PERSECUTION

Then there was the second problem. Ever since Jesus had been put to death as a political threat to the Romans and as a religious threat to the Jews, the danger had existed that his followers would be looked on in the same way. Obviously, those who claimed as their leader one who had died a criminal's death would be suspected of being criminals as well. That kind of attitude toward Christians was apparently on the increase in Mark's time, and some of them were folding under the pressure. Yet if Jesus the Master had suffered, would that not also be the fate of those who saw in him God's final act of mercy for all humanity? If only the followers of Jesus could understand that such suffering, painful as it was, was not their final fate, as it had not been for Jesus. After suffering, they would find joy in God's kingdom. Yet somehow Christians had to be made aware of the fact that there was no safe and easy way for true followers of Jesus. Before he was raised, Jesus suffered the agonizing death of crucifixion. The author of Mark was convinced that the way of the cross was the only path to glory. If that was overlooked, or forgotten, there would be no more true followers of Jesus. There would be no more church worthy of the name. Somehow that point had to be gotten across.

VARIED INTERPRETATIONS OF JESUS

The third problem was closely related to the second. Not everyone who knew about Jesus was persuaded that he had to be understood so exclusively in the light of his passion. After all, hadn't he done some very miraculous things during his lifetime? Hadn't he attracted great crowds with his teaching in Galilee? Hadn't he risen from the dead, so that those who followed him could also expect to share in that resurrection, and heavenly glory? There were all kinds of stories about Jesus in circulation, telling about the things he had done and said. The problem was, people were interpreting these individual stories and sayings in ways that suited their own opinions. Stories of Jesus were being used to justify what people wanted to do and to believe, rather than to teach people what they ought to believe and how they ought to act. It was clear that these individual stories about Jesus, however true they might be in themselves, were no longer sufficient to teach people about him.

We can get a firsthand look at this problem from the letters of St. Paul. He had preached about Jesus Christ, crucified and risen, to the people of the Greek city of Corinth. He had quoted some teachings of Jesus in that preaching, and he had told some stories about him, too. Later on, when he wrote to the Christians there, he reminded them of some of those stories and sayings (1 Co 15:1–7). The trouble was, those stories could so easily be misinterpreted. For example, the Corinthians knew about the Eucharist. They had heard that the Eucharist celebrated Jesus, whom God had raised from the dead. So they celebrated it, but they did so in such a way that it became a wild party, with people drinking so much they got drunk (1 Co 11:21–22). Clearly, such behavior had nothing to do with the Eucharist, and St. Paul let them know that in no uncertain terms. Yet as long as the stories about Jesus were circulating by themselves, they were open to just such misunderstanding.

There are other examples of this problem. People who were interested in magic saw in Jesus' miracles evidence he was a great magician. Maybe if they studied about him, they could gain some of that power (see Ac 8:9–19). People who were interested in philosophy thought perhaps Jesus was another teacher of philosophy, perhaps cleverer than the run-of-the-mill philosophers they ran into, so they tried to learn his philosophical tricks (see Ac 17:18–21). How could the stories about Jesus be protected from such misuse and misunderstanding?

MARK'S SOLUTION

Such were the problems that faced the author of the Gospel of Mark. How could they be solved? The solution our author hit upon was novel. He would put together a large number of the stories about Jesus in such a way that the order in which they were told would help to show how they were to be understood. He would arrange them in such a way that the climax of Jesus' life—the cross and the resurrection—became the climax of the story about Jesus. He would write down the story of Jesus in such a way that everything Jesus said and did led up to his passion, so that any interpretation of Jesus that left the passion out of account would be wrong. To do that, the author of Mark had to create a new literary form that we have come to call "gospel."

When our author wrote his "gospel," therefore, he set out to weave, from the familiar traditions, a tapestry of the life of Jesus which would give a perspective on the traditions he used, and which would also give a perspective on the problems faced by the Christians of his time and place. What is really remarkable is how much the author relied on the traditions he had. For the most part, aside from providing links between the various stories (e.g., 2:1, 13; 4:1–2; 5:21; 6:1) and composing an occasional summary (1:32–34; 3:7–12; 6:53–56), our author made his point by the way he arranged and juxtaposed traditions. Sometimes he would sandwich one tradition into another (e.g., 5:21–43; 11:12–25), so that they could be read together and interpret each other. At other times he would make his point by the order in which he placed them (e.g., 3:20–35 followed by 4:1–12, where we see in family and Pharisees examples of those who observe but do not understand what Jesus is all about). In these and similar ways, the author of Mark seems to have wanted to let the traditions do the talking, as it were, limiting his work to arranging them and putting them into a narrative that climaxed in Jesus' passion.

EMPHASIS ON THE PASSION

The author of Mark laid emphasis on the passion as the key to understanding Jesus in a variety of ways. It is clear throughout the Gospel, for example, that the disciples simply did not understand who Jesus really was. Time and again, they betrayed their inability to grasp the meaning of what Jesus said, and what that meant for who he was. Yet it is also clear that this was due to more than mere stupidity or human failure. They were not *meant* to understand who Jesus was dur-

ing his time with them (cf. 6:52). Mark is dealing here
not with human failure but with God's plan for the salvation of humanity. The key to that plan is the death
and resurrection of Jesus. Therefore, only *after* those
events have occurred will Jesus be able to be understood for what he really is, and only then will anyone
fully understand what he had to say. Mark 9:9 is a
clear example. There Jesus himself makes clear that his
true nature (revealed in the story of the transfiguration,
9:2–8) is not to be revealed until after his resurrection.

The same point is made in other ways—for example,
by the order in which the traditions are given. Thus,
each of the passion predictions is followed by evidence
that the disciples have understood neither what that
meant for Jesus nor what it meant for them (chapters
8, 9, 10). Again, Jesus regularly forbade the demons to
announce who he was. Our author tells us why that was
so. The demons knew who Jesus was (1:34). For people without the supernatural knowledge possessed by
demons, however, Jesus' identity could only really be
understood after his passion.

The emphasis on Jesus' passion probably stems from
the fact that people of that time were attempting to understand Jesus in ways which did not make clear that
the passion was the key to Jesus' career, as we mentioned earlier. The author of Mark was apparently trying to make clear that no one, not even the disciples
who lived and traveled with him for months on end,
could understand Jesus apart from the passion. Mark's
Gospel is therefore a warning. Any attempt to understand Jesus apart from his passion will inevitably fall
into error. The mystery of who Jesus really was
(scholars call it the "messianic secret") cannot be pen-
etrated until God himself lifts the veil by raising him
from the dead.

The Gospel of Mark is therefore not only an attempt to tell the story of Jesus in a new format, namely as a story whose climax is the passion. It is also an attempt to make the theological point that just as the passion was the climax of Jesus' historical life, so it is the climax and key to any attempt to understand him. If the path to glory leads through the vale of the cross, so does the path to knowledge about Jesus. He was not a magician or a philosopher or even primarily a teacher. He was God's Son, who by his suffering and death redeemed humanity (10:45).

UNDERSTANDING THE FALL OF JERUSALEM

Our author solved the problem of the fall of Jerusalem and the burning of the Temple in a similar way. There were a number of traditions about the meaning of the fall of Jerusalem in circulation. Perhaps someone had even written a short tract about it. The author of Mark took these traditions and interspersed comments on them in such a way that it became clear that that cataclysm did not mean Jesus was about to return. In fact, it is impossible to figure out when Jesus will come, because that is known only to God. Christians rather are to remain alert in their faith, but are not to assume that Jerusalem's fall means Jesus' return is now at hand.

WHERE THE GOSPEL WAS WRITTEN

Such interest in the fall of Jerusalem does not mean that Mark lived near that city, or that he was writing his Gospel for people of Jewish descent. The conquest of Jerusalem was so important that the general who ac-

complished it, Titus (who later became an emperor of
Rome), built a triumphal arch in Rome to commemo-
rate his victory. Interest in the event therefore spread
far beyond the boundaries of Palestine. Again, the fact
that Mark had to translate Aramaic phrases into Greek
(e.g., in 5:41 and 7:34) and explain Jewish customs to
his readers (e.g., in 7:3-4) indicates he was writing to
people who knew little if anything about either the language or the customs of Palestine. As we will see in a
moment, Mark's information about the geography of
Palestine was so sketchy that it is hard to believe that
he grew up, or even ever lived, there. Although a later
tradition says our Gospel was written in Rome by an
interpreter of Peter, that seems to be little more than a
guess intended to supply some missing information.

LACK OF CONSISTENT HISTORICAL FRAMEWORK

There are some other characteristics of the Gospel of
Mark that are worth noting. The author was apparently
so intent on pursuing theological goals when he composed his narrative that he did not pay attention to
some of the historical details we would expect in a
story about Jesus. But then, he was not writing a "history" of Jesus. His purpose in constructing the Gospel
was to provide a framework within which individual
traditions about Jesus could find their correct interpretation. As a result, he was not always careful about
time sequences—i.e., when one day or week or month
ended and another began. In most cases he simply put
one tradition after another, with only the simplest kind
of introductory phrases: "in those days," or "after

some days," or simply "again." When he did give times of day, he did not always follow up on them. After telling us it was evening in 4:35, he does not mention any time again until 6:2, when we learn it was the Sabbath. Obviously, not everything reported between 4:35 and 6:2 could have happened in one night. Several days must have passed, but Mark doesn't tell us how many. We can guess if we want, but then we can no longer say we are getting that information from the Gospel of Mark. So any attempt we make to write a "life of Jesus" which seeks to give a day by day, or even month by month, account of his activities will for the most part be based on our guesses rather than on information from Mark.

LACK OF CONSISTENT GEOGRAPHICAL FRAMEWORK

The same thing is true about the reports of Jesus' travels. The author of Mark occasionally tells us where Jesus was at a given time or where he went, but, as in the case of time, these indications of geography are casual and intermittent. In some cases, they are all but unbelievable. For example, the geographical route outlined in 7:31 is much more difficult in the Greek than most English translations are willing to show. Traveling from Tyre to the Sea of Galilee by way of Sidon and the Decapolis would be roughly comparable to traveling from Philadelphia to Washington, D.C., by way of New York City and central Pennsylvania. Even worse, the Greek says the Sea of Galilee is in the "middle of" the Decapolis, when in reality it lies at the very northwest corner of that area. Either Mark was unfamiliar with the geography of Palestine (did you know Sidon is north of Tyre?) or he simply did not care much whether his geography was accurate or not. In either case, we cannot use the geographical references he gave to retrace the travels of Jesus. Again, if we try, most of it will have to be based on guesswork.

HOW TO READ MARK

Once Mark had achieved the theological breakthrough of arranging independent traditions about Jesus' acts and teachings into the format of a story climaxing with the passion, those who followed him could then give more attention to that kind of detail. The authors of both Matthew and Luke used Mark's Gospel in writing their own; if you compare them, you will see how time and again these two authors smoothed out the rough places in Mark and gave the story a smoother flow. But that is due in most cases to their desire to improve Mark's narrative, and not to any superior knowledge they might have had of the actual history of Jesus.

If we want to understand the Gospel of Mark, therefore, we will have to read it for what it is, namely a story that wants to tell us about the religious meaning of Jesus. In doing that, it does not intend to give us accurate historical information about the course of Jesus' life. What it wants us to learn is "gospel truth," not historical truth.

There are one or two other things we will also have to pay attention to if we are going to understand what the Gospel of Mark wants to tell us. For example, we must read Mark carefully and all by itself. We are so accustomed to having all four Gospels that we tend to read any one of them in the light of the other three. Yet when Mark was written, there was no such thing as another Gospel. Matthew, Luke, and John were all written later. Therefore, we must resist the temptation to add to Mark's narrative some of the additional details furnished by one of the other Gospels. That will only confuse our attempt to understand what *Mark* is saying. Reading Mark that way will take a real effort and close concentration, but it is the only way we can get at what it is trying to say rather than what we think it ought to say. Only by concentrating on Mark, and in some cases limiting ourselves to the information Mark alone provides, will we really be able to understand its message.

IMPORTANCE OF STUDYING MARK

As in most worthwhile things, the study of the Gospel of Mark—or of any book in the Bible, for that matter—is not always as easy as we might like. Yet it is surely worth the effort. It will demand careful reading and hard thinking, but the rewards will be great. We have the chance, in reading Mark, to study the product of one of the towering figures in the history of religious literature. He not only created a kind of literature—a "gospel"—but he put a stamp on the understanding of the Christian faith which endures to this day. We owe the fact that we think about Jesus in terms of his life, which led to and climaxed in his passion, to the theological genius of this unknown author, so modest he did not even tell us who he was. In the pages that follow in this commentary, we will try to think that author's thoughts about Jesus after him, to see what they will teach us about ourselves and our faith. Any such exploration means high adventure, and hard work, and it is to such a task that this book invites you.

EDITOR'S NOTE: Sometimes there is a discrepancy between the numbering of chapters and verses in The Jerusalem Bible and that in some other versions. In such cases The Jerusalem Bible citation is given first, followed by the alternative citation—e.g., Ml 3:23 (= 4:5).

Jesus Appears, Preaching the Kingdom of God with Power
Mark 1:1 to 3:6

Mark 1:1–13
BEGINNINGS: JOHN THE BAPTIST

1:1–8
The Gospel begins with John the Baptist

¹ **1** The beginning of the Good News about Jesus
² Christ, the Son of God. ·It is written in the
book of the prophet Isaiah:

> Look, I am going to send my messenger before
> you;
> he will prepare your way.
> ³ A voice cries in the wilderness:
> Prepare a way for the Lord,
> make his paths straight,

⁴ and so it was that John the Baptist appeared in
the wilderness, proclaiming a baptism of repent-
⁵ ance for the forgiveness of sins. ·All Judaea and
all the people of Jerusalem made their way to
him, and as they were baptized by him in the
⁶ river Jordan they confessed their sins. ·John wore
a garment of camel skin, and he lived on locusts
⁷ and wild honey. ·In the course of his preaching
he said, "Someone is following me, someone who
is more powerful than I am, and I am not fit to
⁸ kneel down and undo the strap of his sandals. ·I
have baptized you with water, but he will baptize
you with the Holy Spirit."

✠

The very first sentence of this Gospel contains a puzzle, because it announces that this is the beginning of the good news (or "gospel") of Jesus. Of course it is; where else would the story begin but at the beginning? Mark had another intention with these words, however. For him, the story of Jesus must begin with John if it is to be told correctly (cf. 11:30–33; how one understands Jesus is linked to how one understands John). That link is more than merely historical. It is grounded in the Old Testament. The verses Mark quoted from Isaiah (actually the first two lines come from Malachi 3:1; this may indicate that Mark got the whole quotation from an early Christian collection of appropriate Old Testament verses about Jesus) are intended to show that when John appeared, the long-awaited final act of God for the salvation of humankind had begun. Later in his book, Malachi identified that last forerunner as Elijah (Ml 3:23 [= 4:5]), and Mark is careful to make that identification too. The description of John in verse 6 closely parallels the description of Elijah in the early Greek version of 2 Kings 1:8; and later on, Mark will report that Jesus identified John as Elijah who was to come (9:13; cf. also Lk 1:17).

There is yet more of the prophet about John. His message of repentance is the familiar prophetic call to return to faithfulness to God, a faithfulness that had characterized Israel's earlier time in the wilderness. Just as Israel had once been faithful in the desert (cf. Jr 2:2–3a), so Israel would finally return to the desert and to faithfulness to God in the last times (cf. Ho 2:16 [= 2:14]). The desert is thus more important theologically than geographically. It makes the point about John that must be made, namely that in him the prophetic message about the final, redemptive times had begun its appearance. Yet John is no more than the be-

ginning. He is not yet the fulfillment. John announced
that someone would follow him who was so immeas-
urably greater that not even the most menial task John
could do for him would be appropriate. Thus John, in
the desert, calls all Israel to repent and be washed clean
of their sins, so they will be ready to greet the one who
will come, who will be clothed in God's own Spirit.

STUDY QUESTION: Is it essential to understand Jesus in
                relation to the Old Testament, or is
                such a relationship to the story of
                Israel just "window dressing"?

1:9–13
Baptized and tempted

9   It was at this time that Jesus came from Naza-
    reth in Galilee and was baptized in the Jordan by
10 John. ·No sooner had he come up out of the water
    than he saw the heavens torn apart and the Spirit,
11 like a dove, descending on him. ·And a voice came
    from heaven, "You are my Son, the Beloved; my
    favor rests on you."
12 Immediately afterward the Spirit drove him out
13 into the wilderness ·and he remained there for
    forty days, and was tempted by Satan. He was
    with the wild beasts, and the angels looked after
    him.

✠

The account of Jesus' baptism by John is almost
surely based on a historical event. It creates too many
theological problems to have been invented. For exam-

ple, John's baptism meant forgiven sins. Did Jesus need that? (Cf. Mt 3:14–15 for one solution.) Whether the details are historical, however, we cannot determine, but they are important for what Mark wants to tell us about Jesus.

The Jewish people of that time mourned the loss of prophets and the silence of God. Now, with Jesus' appearance, the heavens were again torn open (cf. Is 63:19b [= 64:1]; Ezk 1:1) and God's Spirit came once more (cf. Is 11:1–2; 61:1; the meaning of the symbolism of the dove for God's Spirit remains unclear). God's voice from heaven drew on language from Psalm 2:7 and Isaiah 42:1, and announced that, like Israel (Ex 4:22; Ho 11:1) or Israel's kings (2 S 7:13–14; Ps 89:20, 26–27), Jesus is now commissioned to fulfill the task of being God's Son.

The Spirit then drove Jesus into the wilderness, the traditional abode of evil and demonic forces, for a test of strength with Satan. Mark thus reveals to us the cosmic dimension of Jesus' earthly ministry. In him, the final climactic battle between God and the powers of evil has been joined. The presence of animals (probably a sign of God's final peace; cf. Is 11:6–9) and angels gives us a hint about who will emerge victorious.

STUDY QUESTIONS: Do you find evidence in our time that this cosmic battle continues? Do you find any hints about the final victor?

Mark 1:14–45
JESUS' MINISTRY INTRODUCED

1:14–20
The time is now

14 After John had been arrested, Jesus went into Galilee. There he proclaimed the Good News
15 from God. ·"The time has come," he said, "and the kingdom of God is close at hand. Repent, and believe the Good News."
16 As he was walking along by the Sea of Galilee he saw Simon and his brother Andrew casting a
17 net in the lake—for they were fishermen. ·And Jesus said to them, "Follow me and I will make you
18 into fishers of men." ·And at once they left their nets and followed him.
19 Going on a little further, he saw James son of Zebedee and his brother John; they too were in their boat, mending their nets. He called them at
20 once ·and, leaving their father Zebedee in the boat with the men he employed, they went after him.

✠

It is clear in these verses that the author of this Gospel has had a hand in shaping them. The language of verses 14–15 comes from a time after Jesus, when the Christian mission had developed some technical theological vocabulary, and the traditions about the first disciples were put together by Mark and placed here in

the narrative. That means our author intends to make
an important theological point in these verses. If we are
to take that point seriously, we must see in everything
that follows verses 14–15 the way the nearness of
God's kingdom manifests itself.

That God's rule over his creation would one day become visible was known in the Old Testament. What is
new here is the statement that now is the time that rule
is to begin. With Jesus' appearance, the kingdom begins
to be visible. In Jesus' words and deeds, the contours of
God's future take on concrete form, and our part in
that future will be determined by how we react to
Jesus. If verses 14–15 are not an actual quotation from
Jesus, they surely represent the substance of what Jesus
said and did, and Mark will make that substance clear
in the rest of his Gospel.

The four disciples whom Jesus called show how one
must react to such news. There is no hint in Mark that
they had known Jesus before (contrast Lk 4:31 to
5:11) or had heard of him through John the Baptist
(contrast Jn 1:35–42). Rather, in exemplary fashion,
they responded to Jesus' call, willing to abandon economic ties (verse 18; cf. 10:21) and even family
(verse 20; cf. 10:28–29, Mt 10:37–38, and Lk
14:26–27) to follow Jesus. That is the way, Mark tells
us, every person ought to respond to the summons of
God's future. That is what it means to "repent and believe the good news."

STUDY QUESTION: We cannot imitate the way the disciples followed the historical Jesus.
What are appropriate ways we can
respond to his summons?

1:21–28
What kind of teacher is this?

²¹   They went as far as Capernaum, and as soon as
      the sabbath came he went to the synagogue and
²² began to teach. ·And his teaching made a deep
      impression on them because, unlike the scribes,
      he taught them with authority.
²³   In their synagogue just then there was a man
      possessed by an unclean spirit, and it shouted,
²⁴ "What do you want with us, Jesus of Nazareth?
      Have you come to destroy us? I know who you are:
²⁵ the Holy One of God." ·But Jesus said sharply, "Be
²⁶ quiet! Come out of him!" ·And the unclean spirit
      threw the man into convulsions and with a loud
²⁷ cry went out of him. ·The people were so aston-
      ished that they started asking each other what it
      all meant. "Here is a teaching that is new," they
      said, "and with authority behind it: he gives or-
      ders even to unclean spirits and they obey him."
²⁸ And his reputation rapidly spread everywhere,
      through all the surrounding Galilean countryside.

✠

The impact this story makes on us is very likely to
be quite different from the impact Mark intended it to
have on his readers. We are likely to be struck primarily by the fact that Jesus cast out an "unclean spirit"
or "demon." Yet such activity was not at all unique to
Jesus at that time. Many wandering exorcists had such
demon-expulsions reported of them, and such stories

had evolved a regular pattern. That pattern is closely followed in our story (verses 23–27a). After the demonic force made its presence felt, often with a formula to gain power over the exorcist (normally by pronouncing his name and further identifying him), the exorcist replied with a counter formula and a command to leave. If the counter formula was successful, the demon was forced to leave, often with visible or audible proof of its exit. The astonishment of bystanders often concluded the story. It is hence quite clear that our story had been told and retold before it came to be placed in Mark's Gospel. It is not the story as such, therefore, that carries Mark's point, but rather the framework into which he put it. That point is no longer Jesus' power over demonic forces, although of course Mark acknowledged that. Rather, the point is now Jesus' power as *teacher*. The material Mark provided to bracket this story (verses 21–22, 27–28) is designed to show us the kind of power and authority Jesus wielded when he taught. The same power that enabled Jesus to force the demonic powers to obey him was also present in his teaching!

It is also noteworthy that Mark chose to report this as the first of the many miracles he would tell of Jesus. Mark thus meant this miracle to indicate the perspective from which all subsequent stories of this kind are to be viewed, namely, that Jesus spoke with the same miraculous power by which he acted. Thus Jesus' power is available to many more than Jesus could affect with his physical presence. Wherever his word is heard, his power is also present, to heal people from the evil forces that disrupt their lives. That is why Mark has identified the story of Jesus as "good news."

STUDY QUESTION: Do you find any indication that Jesus' words still carry such healing power, even in our world?

1:29–34
Where Jesus is, healing happens

29 On leaving the synagogue, he went with James and John straight to the house of Simon and An-
30 drew. ·Now Simon's mother-in-law had gone to bed with fever, and they told him about her
31 straightaway. ·He went to her, took her by the hand and helped her up. And the fever left her and she began to wait on them.
32 That evening, after sunset, they brought to him all who were sick and those who were possessed
33 by devils. ·The whole town came crowding around
34 the door, ·and he cured many who were suffering from diseases of one kind or another; he also cast out many devils, but he would not allow them to speak, because they knew who he was.

✠

The simple, straightforward story of the healing of Peter's mother-in-law, cast in the form the oral tradition gave to all such stories, further confirms the importance of the first four disciples Jesus called. Peter, James, and John, sometimes with Andrew, were often present with Jesus when the remaining twelve were not (5:37; 9:2; 13:3). Yet even these most intimate disciples show how hard it is to come to terms with Jesus as God's Son (cf. 10:35–37; 14:66–72).

Because verses 32–34 depend on their present context (the Sabbath mentioned in verse 21 is over at sunset, so people can gather around the door of the house
mentioned in verse 29), either the material contained
in verses 23–34 circulated as a unit before Mark wrote
it down, or else, more likely, verses 32–34 were composed by Mark as a summary of the kind of activity of
Jesus he has been reporting. With these verses, Mark
tells us that Jesus' healing ministry was far more exten-
sive than he has space to report. Verse 34 has a further
point, however. Jesus' command silencing the unclean
spirit in verse 25, there simply part of the normal procedure in telling about an exorcism, here gains a new
interpretation. That command is now understood to
imply Jesus' desire to keep his true identity unknown
(cf. 3:11–12). But then why did Jesus do such things
in public? There is more to it than simply Jesus' desire
to avoid publicity, however. Mark points here for the
first time to a dimension of mystery that will become
increasingly important to his narrative. At this point,
the nature of that mystery remains unclear.

1:35–39
A matter of priorities

35 　In the morning, long before dawn, he got up
and left the house, and went off to a lonely place
36 and prayed there. ·Simon and his companions set
37 out in search for him, ·and when they found him
38 they said, "Everybody is looking for you." ·He
answered, "Let us go elsewhere, to the neighbor-
ing country towns, so that I can preach there too,

³⁹ because that is why I came." ·And he went all through Galilee, preaching in their synagogues and casting out devils.

✠

It is clear from the details in verse 35 that Mark intended us to link this story with the preceding stories which told us about a day's activity of Jesus in Capernaum. That activity had been enormously successful, and the crowds were clamoring for another day like it. Yet Jesus chose to withdraw, first for prayer, and then to go to other regions. He had been sent to announce the nearness of God's final rule, and success, or even human need, could not detain him from spreading that announcement. Jesus did not decide to give up healing for preaching. That is clear from verse 39. He simply could not stay in one place, for whatever reason, since his mission was to spread abroad the good news of God's coming kingdom. Yet verse 39 has further significance. Because Mark tells us Jesus not only preached but also overcame the demonic forces of evil, he will not let us lose the larger perspective against which we must understand the activities of Jesus as itinerant preacher and wonder-worker. Jesus is part of God's final, cosmic battle against the powers of evil. To miss that point is to miss the meaning of Jesus.

STUDY QUESTIONS: Does Mark mean all disciples are to follow Jesus' model of being itinerant, or is the case of Jesus special? Is there a place for an ongoing announcement of God's coming rule in Jesus?

1:40–45
Jesus conquers leprosy

40   A leper came to him and pleaded on his knees: "If you want to," he said, "you can cure me."
41   Feeling sorry for him, Jesus stretched out his hand and touched him. "Of course I want to!"
42   he said. "Be cured!" ·And the leprosy left him at
43   once and he was cured. ·Jesus immediately sent
44   him away and sternly ordered him, ·"Mind you say nothing to anyone, but go and show yourself to the priest, and make the offering for your healing prescribed by Moses as evidence of your re-
45   covery." ·The man went away, but then started talking about it freely and telling the story everywhere, so that Jesus could no longer go openly into any town, but had to stay outside in places where nobody lived. Even so, people from all around would come to him.

✠

This is a puzzling story. There is a well-attested tradition in the ancient Greek manuscripts that instead of Jesus "feeling sorry for" the leper, Jesus is angered (at the demonic forces that produce disease?). "Sent him away" in verse 43 translates the same word as that used at the end of verse 39 to describe the expulsion of demons; it literally means "cast him out." The word rendered "sternly ordered" in the same verse is a term used to describe the snorting of a war horse in battle; such "snorting" was part of the technique of contemporary wonder-workers. What are we to make of all that?

Two points, at least, are clear. First, Jesus is a man possessed by God, and is strange even in his own world. To reduce him to a sentimental "friend in the garden" is blasphemous. To confront him is to confront the living God. The only proper attitude is that of the leper, who says "if *you* want to, you can cure me." We are God's creatures, not his buddies. Second, this is a climactic act of Jesus. Leprosy made the victim a total outcast (see Lv 13:45–46), and religious Jews regarded the victims as the "living dead." To cure leprosy was equivalent to raising the dead.

It is small wonder that, however hard he may have tried, Jesus could not keep from notoriety (verse 45). The problem is the very human desire to have God at our disposal, so we can use his power the way we want to. It is that human desire that hounded Jesus and, frustrated, nailed him to a cross. God is not always welcomed in his world.

STUDY QUESTIONS: Does some of our piety conceal a desire to bend God to our will? What should be the Christian's attitude to God's power?

Mark 2:1 to 3:6
CONFLICT WITH RELIGIOUS AUTHORITIES

2:1–12
Who does this man think he is?

1 When he returned to Capernaum some time later, word went around that he was back; 2 and so many people collected that there was no room left, even in front of the door. He was 3 preaching the word to them ·when some people came bringing him a paralytic carried by four 4 men, ·but as the crowd made it impossible to get the man to him, they stripped the roof over the place where Jesus was; and when they had made an opening, they lowered the stretcher on which 5 the paralytic lay. ·Seeing their faith, Jesus said to the paralytic, "My child, your sins are forgiven." 6 Now some scribes were sitting there, and they 7 thought to themselves, ·"How can this man talk like that? He is blaspheming. Who can forgive 8 sins but God?" ·Jesus, inwardly aware that this was what they were thinking, said to them, "Why do you have these thoughts in your hearts? 9 Which of these is easier: to say to the paralytic, 'Your sins are forgiven' or to say, 'Get up, pick 10 up your stretcher and walk'? ·But to prove to you that the Son of Man has authority on earth to for- 11 give sins,"—·he said to the paralytic—"I order you: get up, pick up your stretcher, and go off home." 12 And the man got up, picked up his stretcher at once and walked out in front of everyone, so that they were all astounded and praised God saying, "We have never seen anything like this."

✠

There is considerable evidence to indicate that at some point in the tradition two independent stories were combined into this one. (1) The "all" in verse 12 who praised God are not likely to have included the opposing scribes (verse 6). (2) The conclusion (verse 12) has no reference at all to the dispute about forgiving sins. (3) There seems to be a break in the story between verses 10 and 11, where a phrase from verse 5 is repeated. (4) We can recover a formally complete miracle story in verses 3–5 and 10b–12, which makes no mention of the discussion in verses 5–10. It therefore appears that this combination of healing and discussion does not reflect a historical event, but is rather the product of the combination of traditions.

The fact that the kind of language that is typical of the material Mark himself wrote is limited to verses 1–2 indicates that the two stories were already combined into a single unit by the time they reached Mark. The unusual use of the title "Son of Man" in verse 10 (in Mark that title ordinarily refers to Jesus' death and is used chiefly in the second half of the Gospel) points in the same direction. Mark thus took the combined stories, gave them an introduction, and placed them at this point in his narrative.

What did such a combination of miracle and dispute accomplish? Clearly, it demonstrated that Jesus' word is effective. Just as lame men walk when Jesus commanded, so are sins forgiven when he forgives. Perhaps it is easier to say "your sins are forgiven." There is no way to know if that actually happened. To say "stand and walk," on the other hand, is to say something whose effects can be observed. In this story, the fact that the paralytic can walk is proof that Jesus' words are effective (we already saw the power-laden nature of Jesus' words in 1:21–28).

That combination also says something about Jesus. The scribes insist that only God can forgive sins (verse 6), something Jesus does not dispute. Yet he then declares sins forgiven! Clearly, Jesus here was understood to be able to act for God. As we shall see, Mark understood the relationship of Jesus to God to be one of action, in which Jesus does what otherwise only God can do.

A further point is worth noting. Faith (verse 5) has nothing to do with the subjective state of the one to be healed, as though it were a necessary precondition. Faith is ascribed to the four who brought the paralytic, and it describes a way of understanding Jesus that translated itself into action. Those four let nothing hinder them from bringing the paralytic to Jesus. That is what "faith" means in this story.

Finally, if healing and forgiveness of sin are so closely related, then Mark may want us to understand that all healings are illustrative of Jesus' restoration of the fellowship between God and humankind which is ruptured by our rebellion against God, with its resulting separation from him. Jesus' "authority" to heal and forgive means that in him, the grace-filled nearness of God's kingdom makes itself felt.

STUDY QUESTIONS: Does Mark mean healing will *always* follow the forgiveness of sin? Can a sick person still believe God has forgiven his or her sins?

2:13–17
Jesus offends some religious people

13   He went out again to the shore of the lake; and
      all the people came to him, and he taught them.
14 As he was walking on he saw Levi the son of
      Alphaeus, sitting by the customs house, and he
      said to him, "Follow me." And he got up and
      followed him.
15   When Jesus was at dinner in his house, a num-
      ber of tax collectors and sinners were also sitting
      at the table with Jesus and his disciples; for there
16 were many of them among his followers. ·When
      the scribes of the Pharisee party saw him eating
      with sinners and tax collectors, they said to his
      disciples, "Why does he eat with tax collectors and
17 sinners?" ·When Jesus heard this he said to them,
      "It is not the healthy who need the doctor, but
      the sick. I did not come to call the virtuous, but
      sinners."

✠

These two stories, perhaps combined and given an
introduction by Mark (verse 13), intend to illustrate
verse 17 (Levi is so unimportant Mark never mentions
him again). Tax-collectors were "sinners" to religious
Jews not only because they served the occupying
Roman government but because their business required
association with ritually impure people. Tax-collectors,
and all others who did not scrupulously follow the
priestly laws of ceremonial purity, were avoided by the
Pharisees. Those Pharisees have often suffered from a
bad press in our day. They were not bad. Their prob-

lem was that they were too religious! They tried to real-
ize the divine command that Israel become "a nation of
priests" (Ex 19:6), and they were so single-minded
about it that they put that ahead of everything else in
life. Whoever didn't put those rules about being as pure
as a priest above everything else, they automatically
branded as sinners. That is why they could only react
with disgust when Jesus wouldn't also keep those rules.
He actually associated with sinners! Worse yet, he
sought them out, and even ate with them. When they
challenged him, he said his task was to seek out the sinners, not associate with the virtuous.

Does that mean there are people virtuous enough not
to need Jesus? Yet who are so well they do not need a
physician if the physician is God himself? Who are so
good they can tell God they do not need his forgiveness? Jesus here acted out God's forgiving attitude
to sinners. God comes to them! Those who think they
are not sinners thus exclude themselves when God
comes to call. That is the price the Pharisees paid for
being so religious.

STUDY QUESTIONS: How is it possible to be "too religious"? Doesn't God like religious
people better than sinners?

2:18–22
Now what about fasting?

18   One day when John's disciples and the Pharisees were fasting, some people came and said to
him, "Why is it that John's disciples and the disciples of the Pharisees fast, but your disciples do

19 not?" ·Jesus replied, "Surely the bridegroom's attendants would never think of fasting while the
bridegroom is still with them? As long as they
have the bridegroom with them, they could not
20 think of fasting. ·But the time will come for the
bridegroom to be taken away from them, and
21 then, on that day, they will fast. ·No one sews a
piece of unshrunken cloth on an old cloak; if he
does, the patch pulls away from it, the new from
22 the old, and the tear gets worse. ·And nobody puts
new wine into old wineskins; if he does, the wine
will burst the skins, and the wine is lost and the
skins too. No! New wine, fresh skins!"

✠

One of the major problems with Jesus was that he
did not act like a religious person should. His refusal to
fast caused problems for all law-abiding Jews. In fact,
he may have even caused difficulties for later Christians
as well, since verses 18–19a seem to mean no fasting at
all, while verses 19b–20 seem to mean no fasting only
while Jesus is physically present. These latter verses almost look like they were put there to justify the later
Christian practice of fasting. Yet the passage closes
with verses 21–22, which again seem to imply that if
you combine the new things Jesus brings with old religious customs (like fasting!) you destroy both. That
seems to mean the same as verses 18–19a, namely, that
the old custom of fasting is out. Maybe verses 19b–20
only want to hint at the sadness Jesus' followers will
feel when he goes to the cross.

Despite such problems, the main point of these
verses is clear. With Jesus something so decisively new
has happened that there is no chance to remain un-
changed by it. With his presence, only joy is appro-

priate, a joy which could only be compared to a wedding time, the happiest of times for Jews of that period.

That joy will be marred by sorrow at his absence. There is still a cross in his future. Yet this much is certain: with Jesus in our midst, the only appropriate reaction is joy.

STUDY QUESTION: What are some appropriate ways for us to share in this joy at the new things Jesus brings?

2:23–28
Don't Sabbath rules mean anything?

23   One sabbath day he happened to be taking a walk through the cornfields, and his disciples be-
24   gan to pick ears of corn as they went along. •And the Pharisees said to him, "Look, why are they doing something on the sabbath day that is for-
25   bidden?" •And he replied, "Did you never read what David did in his time of need when he and
26   his followers were hungry—•how he went into the house of God when Abiathar was high priest, and ate the loaves of offering which only the priests are allowed to eat, and how he also gave some to the men with him?"
27   And he said to them, "The sabbath was made
28   for man, not man for the sabbath; •so the Son of Man is master even of the sabbath."

✠

According to the gospel evidence, it was characteristic of Jesus to disregard the multitude of Jewish legalities limiting activity on the Sabbath (our Saturday). This story presented one defense of that disregard.

Mark's Greek does not indicate that the disciples ate the grain they picked; it implies they picked it as part of making their path through the grainfield. Nor is their hunger mentioned anywhere. That is a detail added later in the Gospels of Matthew and Luke to conform to a detail about David's followers (verse 25). Jesus' defense is therefore not to enunciate a different law— e.g., "human necessity supersedes Sabbath legalisms," the necessity here being hunger. Rather, as verse 28 makes clear, the defense is based on who Jesus is. The comparison Jesus draws in verses 25–26 is between himself and David. Jesus, the lowly carpenter of Nazareth (so he appeared to the Pharisees), here put himself on a par with King David. What David, as God's anointed could do, that Jesus may also do.

The final two verses confirm that point. They apparently circulated as a saying of Jesus independently of this story (and were probably added to this story by Mark, who used his characteristic phrase "and he said to them" to connect them). Those verses made the point that because man is more important than the Sabbath, he is free to act as he sees fit (for the parallel use of "man" and "Son of Man," cf. Ps 8:4; both lines make the same point, as here). In this context, however, the verses point to the importance of Jesus. He, as Son of Man is (like God!) Lord of the Sabbath. The story is clear evidence of Mark's high Christology.

STUDY QUESTION: Do we, as followers of Jesus, have the same freedom in regard to rules about Sunday?

3:1–6
Jesus, the law-breaker, heals

1 3 He went again into a synagogue, and there
2 was a man there who had a withered hand.
And they were watching him to see if he would
cure him on the sabbath day, hoping for some-
3 thing to use against him. ·He said to the man with
the withered hand, "Stand up out in the middle!"
4 Then he said to them, "Is it against the law on
the sabbath day to do good, or to do evil; to save
5 life, or to kill?" But they said nothing. ·Then,
grieved to find them so obstinate, he looked an-
grily around at them, and said to the man, "Stretch
out your hand." He stretched it out and his hand
6 was better. ·The Pharisees went out and at once
began to plot with the Herodians against him, dis-
cussing how to destroy him.

☩

This is the fifth of the stories (beginning with 2:1)
that detail mounting opposition to Jesus. It is once
more the Sabbath, Jesus is faced with a potential healing, and his opponents wait to pounce. In cases of mor-
tal danger, even Pharisees allowed appropriate rescue
operations on the Sabbath, but this man was in no mor-
tal danger. Jesus could wait until the Sabbath was over
to restore the hand. Yet, as Jesus' question (verse 4)
showed, the real issue was, is it unlawful to do good on
the Sabbath? His opponents' spying presence indicated
they would have to answer yes to that question. Even

more, as verse 6 indicates, they are seeking a reason, on the Sabbath, to kill him. Thus their actions show they would also have to answer yes to the question, is it lawful to do evil on the Sabbath? Thus the law, as it is here applied by the Pharisees, forbids doing good and allows doing evil on the Sabbath. What a perversion of God's law! By this confrontation, and by his act of healing, Jesus made clear that the Pharisaic interpretation of the law has negated God's will as it is expressed in that law. That is the whole problem with the ultrareligious Pharisees. In the name of religion, they pervert the goal of religion.

In this incident Jesus offered the Pharisees an opportunity to see the box into which they had placed themselves, using the law to defeat the intention of the law. They did not take the opportunity. Faced with the choice between their laws and Jesus, they chose their laws, and sought to put mercy to death.

STUDY QUESTIONS: Do all religious rules eventually eliminate a place for mercy? Can rules and mercy ever exist side by side?

Jesus' Ministry in Galilee,
and His Rejection by His Own
Mark 3:7 to 6:6

Mark 3:7–35
TRUE FOLLOWERS OF JESUS

3:7–12
The crowds respond

7 Jesus withdrew with his disciples to the lakeside, and great crowds from Galilee followed him.
8 From Judaea, ·Jerusalem, Idumaea, Transjordania
and the region of Tyre and Sidon, great numbers
who had heard of all he was doing came to him.
9 And he asked his disciples to have a boat ready
for him because of the crowd, to keep him from
10 being crushed. ·For he had cured so many that
all who were afflicted in any way were crowding
11 forward to touch him. ·And the unclean spirits,
whenever they saw him, would fall down before
12 him and shout, "You are the Son of God!" ·But
he warned them strongly not to make him known.

✠

Style and language make it clear that Mark is largely
responsible for the present shape of these verses. With
this summary, a new segment begins which reaches to
6:6, where, like the previous segment (1:1 to 3:6), it
ends with rejection of Jesus. Placed here, these verses
contrast the reaction of common people from a wide
area with that of the official religious establishment in
the preceding verse (3:6).

It is clear that Mark understands the popularity of Jesus to be due to his reputation as a wonder-worker. The crowds were attracted by "all he was doing"; they threaten to crush him in reaction to the healing he continued to do; and he faced again the problem of unclean spirits identifying him (cf. 1:34). Verses 11–12 do constitute a problem. Jesus' unwillingness to let unclean spirits "make him known" can have nothing to do with any notion Mark may have had that Jesus didn't want to be known as a miracle-worker. Verse 10 makes that impossible. Nor can it be due to any supposed desire by Jesus to avoid publicity. He made no effort here to escape the crowds, only to keep them from crushing him. Perhaps it is not appropriate for demons to tell who Jesus really is, namely not just another wonder-worker but God's Son, or perhaps the time had not yet come when people would understand correctly what that meant.

STUDY QUESTIONS: Why would it be inappropriate for unclean spirits to make Jesus known as Son of God? Can a correct identification of Jesus ever be out of place?

3:13–19
Twelve are appointed

¹³   He now went up into the hills and summoned
¹⁴   those he wanted. So they came to him ·and he ap-
     pointed twelve; they were to be his companions

¹⁵ and to be sent out to preach, ·with power to cast
¹⁶ out devils. ·And so he appointed the Twelve: Si-
¹⁷ mon to whom he gave the name Peter, ·James the
     son of Zebedee and John the brother of James, to
     whom he gave the name Boanerges or "Sons of
¹⁸ Thunder"; ·then Andrew, Philip, Bartholomew,
     Matthew, Thomas, James the son of Alphaeus,
¹⁹ Thaddaeus, Simon the Zealot ·and Judas Iscariot,
     the man who was to betray him.

☩

The order of stories here in Mark implies that it was
as a response to his rejection by religious authorities and
his popularity as wonder-worker that Jesus created
an inner circle of twelve, who were to accompany him
and share his ministry (verses 14–15; cf. 1:38, 39).
The location in the hills (in Greek, literally "the
mountain") has theological rather than geographic
significance. Just as God on Mount Sinai made Israel
his people, so now Jesus on a mountain constituted,
through these twelve, the new Israel. That the number,
not the men themselves, is important is shown by the
fact that, while the number twelve is constant throughout the New Testament, the names of the men vary
among the Gospels (compare the list here and in Mt
10:2–4 with Lk 6:14–16 and Ac 1:13; John has
names mentioned in no other Gospel). Similarly, the
first three men in the list are given new names, not because of their personal character (for Peter, see 8:33
and 14:66–72; for James and John, see 10:35–37) but
because they will now play a significant role in God's
plan of salvation (cf. Abram/Abraham, Gn 17:5, and
Jacob/Israel, Gn 32:29 [= 32:28] and 35:10 for
similar instances). Peter's importance in all such lists

may rest on remembrance that he was the first of the
apostles to see the risen Jesus (cf. 1 Co 15:5). Perhaps
for that reason, his calling as disciple is also recorded
first (1:16; cf. Lk 5:1–11). Finally, the fact that many
of those named here played no recorded role in the
subsequent life of the church and the fact that the betrayer is included in their number indicate that the
choice of the twelve did originate with Jesus, rather
than with the later church as an attempt to justify its
form of government.

STUDY QUESTION: If the number twelve implies that
the followers of Jesus constitute the
new Israel, what does that say
about the ongoing relationship between the church and the people of
Israel?

3:20–30
Jesus is a source of confusion

20   He went home again, and once more such a
crowd collected that they could not even have a
21   meal. ·When his relatives heard of this, they set
out to take charge of him, convinced he was out
of his mind.
22   The scribes who had come down from Jerusalem were saying, "Beelzebul is in him" and, "It
is through the prince of devils that he casts devils
23   out." ·So he called them to him and spoke to them
24   in parables, "How can Satan cast out Satan? ·If a
kingdom is divided against itself, that kingdom
25   cannot last. ·And if a household is divided against

26 itself, that household can never stand. ·Now if
Satan has rebelled against himself and is divided,
27 he cannot stand either—it is the end of him. ·But
no one can make his way into a strong man's
house and burgle his property unless he has tied
up the strong man first. Only then can he burgle
his house.
28 "I tell you solemnly, all men's sins will be for-
29 given, and all their blasphemies; ·but let anyone
blaspheme against the Holy Spirit and he will
never have forgiveness: he is guilty of an eternal
30 sin." ·This was because they were saying, "An unclean spirit is in him."

✠

Mark describes again the contrast between the
masses who respond to Jesus and the small groups who
reject him. The irony is that precisely those who ought
to have recognized his importance, his family and the
religious authorities, not only failed to recognize it but
instead openly rejected it. If, as seems likely, Mark has
put these traditions into their present order, he has pronounced a hard judgment on Jesus' family—namely,
that their attitude to Jesus is comparable to that of the
scribes. This is evidence that members of Jesus' family were not among those who followed him prior to his
resurrection (cf. Jn 7:5).

Mark begins with the relatives, and then shifts to detail objections of the scribes. The discussion of the
family is completed in verses 31–35, thus bracketing
the material about the scribes. Jesus' response to the
accusation that he controls devils through devilish
power is given in "parables." This is the first occurrence of that word in Mark. He will give extended examples in chapter 4. Parables require some com-

monality between speaker and listener to be
understood. To those who have no sympathy with Jesus
or his claims, they make little sense (cf. 4:10–12).
Characteristically, these parables do not illustrate time-
less moral truths. Rather, they explain the kind of
conflict in which Jesus is engaged. We may thus expect
subsequent parables to pursue the same goal of giving
perspective on Jesus and his mission.

The point of verses 23–26 is not entirely clear. Perhaps they are intended to say that if Jesus operated by
the prince of devils in casting other devils out, Satan is
shown to be divided and powerless, something patently
false. Or perhaps they mean to say that whatever you
think of the source of Jesus' power, what he does shows
that Satan no longer has the upper hand. The climax in
verse 27 is clear enough, however. Jesus is the stronger
one, who controls devils not as their prince but as their
conqueror (cf. Is 49:24–25, where the stronger one is
God himself).

Verse 30 is the key to the meaning of verses 28–29.
The one limitation on God's limitless forgiveness of sin
is to insist that Jesus' authority is from Satan rather
than from God, as the scribes had just done. That
means that if Jesus incarnates God's forgiveness of sin
(cf. 2:17; 10:45), then the unforgivable sin is to reject
that forgiveness, by rejecting Jesus. To refuse Jesus is
to refuse God's forgiveness. For such a refusal, obviously no forgiveness remains. The key, therefore, is
Jesus. To accept him is to be accepted (forgiven) by
God. To reject him is to reject God (and his forgiveness) as well.

STUDY QUESTIONS: Is there any modern equivalent to
                    the claim that it is Satan, not

God's Spirit, that is at work in Jesus? Is the emphasis here more on a sin that can't be forgiven (verse 29), or on the overwhelming grace that forgives "all men's sins" (verse 28)?

3:31–35
Who belongs to Jesus' true family?

31 His mother and brothers now arrived and, standing outside, sent in a message asking for him.
32 A crowd was sitting around him at the time the message was passed to him, "Your mother and brothers and sisters are outside asking for you."
33 He replied, "Who are my mother and my broth-
34 ers?" ·And looking around at those sitting in a circle about him, he said, "Here are my mother
35 and my brothers. ·Anyone who does the will of God, that person is my brother and sister and mother."

✠

The form of this story indicates that it circulated in the tradition as an independent unit before Mark put it in his Gospel. Its point is not so much the exclusion of his relatives as the wider inclusion into his family of all who follow him. Blood descent is no longer enough to qualify one for inclusion in God's redemptive family. Perhaps that is a hint that inclusion among those favored by God no longer depends on racial descent, as it did in Judaism. The position of verse 35 after verse 34 makes it clear that they do God's will who hear Jesus. That kind of claim was bound to offend pious people who found little in Jesus to fit their expectation of the final divine redeemer of Israel.

It is that offense inherent in Jesus that Mark has emphasized by placing this originally independent story into this context. By placing accounts of Jesus' relatives before and after the scribes' negative judgment on Jesus, Mark gives the attitude of Jesus' family a negative interpretation. Jesus is so unexpected, so strange in his own world, that even those in a position to know most about him (family) and his religious claims (scribes) are offended in him.

STUDY QUESTION: Are there elements in Jesus' actions and words that continue to be offensive to those who know him best?

Mark 4:1–34
AND HE TAUGHT THEM MANY THINGS IN PARABLES

4:1–20
Parables and the meaning of Jesus

¹ 4 Again he began to teach by the lakeside, but such a huge crowd gathered around him that he got into a boat on the lake and sat there. The people were all along the shore, at the water's ² edge. ·He taught them many things in parables, and in the course of his teaching he said to them, ³⁄₄ "Listen! Imagine a sower going out to sow. ·Now it happened that, as he sowed, some of the seed fell on the edge of the path, and the birds came ⁵ and ate it up. ·Some seed fell on rocky ground where it found little soil and sprang up straight- ⁶ away, because there was no depth of earth; ·and when the sun came up it was scorched and, not ⁷ having any roots, it withered away. ·Some seed fell into thorns, and the thorns grew up and ⁸ choked it, and it produced no crop. ·And some seeds fell into rich soil and, growing tall and strong, produced crop; and yielded thirty, sixty, ⁹ even a hundredfold." ·And he said, "Listen, any- one who has ears to hear!"

¹⁰ When he was alone, the Twelve, together with the others who formed his company, asked what ¹¹ the parables meant. ·He told them, "The secret of the kingdom of God is given to you, but to those who are outside everything comes in para-

¹² bles, ·so that they may see and see again, but not
perceive; may hear and hear again, but not understand; otherwise they might be converted and be
forgiven."

¹³   He said to them, "Do you not understand this
parable? Then how will you understand any of the
¹⁴ parables? ·What the sower is sowing is the word.
¹⁵ Those on the edge of the path where the word is
sown are people who have no sooner heard it than
Satan comes and carries away the word that was
¹⁶ sown in them. ·Similarly, those who receive the
seed on patches of rock are people who, when
first they hear the word, welcome it at once with
¹⁷ joy. ·But they have no root in them, they do not
last; should some trial come, or some persecution
on account of the word, they fall away at once.
¹⁸ Then there are others who receive the seed in
¹⁹ thorns. These have heard the word, ·but the wor-
ries of this world, the lure of riches and all the
other passions come in to choke the word, and so
²⁰ it produces nothing. ·And there are those who
have received the seed in rich soil: they hear the
word and accept it and yield a harvest, thirty and
sixty and a hundredfold."

✞

A preliminary consideration may help to dispel some
of the problems regularly encountered in attempting to
understand these verses. We are dealing here with
parables, not allegories. In an allegory, something already known is put into a kind of code, and every element in the allegory stands for something else. Revelation 17:1–6 is a good example. It is really a description
of ancient Rome, but it is disguised as the description
of a woman. An allegory therefore tells familiar things
in a strange, coded form. A parable on the other hand
is a story about familiar things, designed to get the lis-

tener to perceive something new. The point of the story as a whole, not its individual details, is intended to apply to the current situation and illumine it. The parable is therefore a story about familiar things that seeks to open a new perspective on the situation of the listener.

Mark's language makes it evident that he has assembled these stories and sayings of 4:1–34 from his traditions. Though his introduction (verses 1–2) specifies that the parable of the sower is only one example of the parables of Jesus (verse 2), it is clearly the key example (verse 13). Misunderstanding here means misunderstanding of all Jesus' parables. Mark framed the parable with two commands to pay attention (the "listen" of verse 3, and verse 9), provided from his tradition two explanations for it (11–12 and 13–20), and then illustrated its point with sayings (21–25) and further parables (26–32). All that shows how important he took it to be.

The agricultural procedure described in the parable was normal enough. Palestinian farmers plowed only after sowing, so seed on paths in the field and among thorns would be plowed under with the rest, and one cannot always tell where the soil lies thin over the limestone shelves common in Galilee (the "rocky ground" of verse 5). The harvest, however, seems to be quite beyond normal expectations. What began as a normal, even somewhat unpromising event results in something astounding. Who could have known, observing the farmer in his ordinary activity, that this time the results would surpass all expectations? The parable contains an implicit warning. To think that that sower was an ordinary sower was proved wrong by the harvest. Don't make the same mistake with Jesus. To account for

Jesus in ordinary terms will be proved wrong by God's
coming kingdom.

Mark reinforces that point in verses 11–12. The parable points to the mystery of the kingdom of God.
Note well, it does not give us further information about
the kingdom. Matthew and Luke interpreted Mark that
way (see Mt 13:11 and Lk 8:10), but Mark does not
say the parable provides us with information about
myster*ies*. Rather the parable points to one mystery,
without which there is only confusion and inability to
repent (verse 12).

What is that mystery, given those who "formed his
company"? It is the link of Jesus to the kingdom. It is
to see in Jesus one in whose words and acts God himself is at work, and then to follow him. Without such a
perspective on Jesus, one will miss the importance of
the events surrounding him, as scribes and family
have just demonstrated (3:20–35). Those who accept
Jesus as the potent herald of God's coming kingdom
("you," verse 11, i.e., those who follow Jesus, verse
10) see in Jesus the key to those events. Those who do
not, find only confusion worse confounded (verse 12).
Explanation and parable point to the same thing: to
Jesus' actions are attached the astonishing results of
God's kingdom. Failure to recognize that importance of
Jesus means failure to understand anything about him.

That is the situation faced by those who hear and see
Jesus. If they accept him as God's sign, they are able to
understand what he does and says. If they reject him,
they find what he says confusing and what he does ob-
jectionable. (Again see 3:20–35; it is not accidental
that Mark has chapter 4 follow that passage!)

Mark appends a second explanation (verses 13–20),
which by vocabulary and content shows it originated as

an early commentary by the Christian community on
this parable. The allegory is not consistent. In verse 14
the seed is the Word, in verse 17 the people who receive
it. Even here, therefore, the intention is not the allegory
as such, but the attempt to make the parable meaning-
ful for a time when the problems outlined in verses
15–19 had become acute. Mark uses this explanation
to reinforce his point once more: those who see and
hear everything Jesus does and says, yet refuse to accept Jesus for what he is, soon become the "outsiders"
described in verse 11. Only those who accept Jesus
(the "good soil" of verse 20) profit from what he says.

In this chapter, then, Mark gives the reason why
some who had seen what Jesus did and said—family
and scribes—still misunderstood him so completely:
they had not recognized his importance for God's kingdom. One faces in Jesus the reality of God's rule. That
is the situation the parables seek to illumine.

STUDY QUESTIONS: Can reports of what Jesus said and
                  did still cause confusion? Can
                  modern parables be found to help
                  illumine our situation vis-à-vis
                  Jesus?

4:21–25
Sayings on the parable's point

21   He also said to them, "Would you bring in
      a lamp to put it under a tub or under the bed?
22 Surely you will put it on the lampstand? ·For

there is nothing hidden but it must be disclosed, nothing kept secret except to be brought to light.
23 If anyone has ears to hear, let him listen to this."
24   He also said to them, "Take notice of what you are hearing. The amount you measure out is the
25 amount you will be given—and more besides; ·for the man who has will be given more; from the man who has not, even what he has will be taken away."

☩

Mark continues here to assemble materials from his traditions. That is shown by the repeated Markan formula "He also said to them" (verses 21, 24), by the phrase about listening (verse 23; cf. verse 9), and by the fact that, though both Matthew and Luke repeat all these sayings, they put them into other contexts, perhaps because they knew they were originally unattached to one another. We can only guess what they meant originally, but Mark makes his intention clear. Like the parable, they warn the listener not to ignore the kingdom's first rays of dawn in Jesus, however unpromising he may seem for such purposes. The strange Greek of verse 21 shows that. Literally, it reads: "Does a lamp come in order to be put under a bushel or under a bed?" But what "lamp" is thus able to "come"? Clearly, it refers to Jesus. Though the light of the kingdom he brings now seems dim or even hidden, it will yet, in its time, become manifest (verse 22). For that reason, special attention must be given to Jesus (verse 23), since one's final reward depends on how one reacts now to Jesus (verse 24; cf. 8:38). Not to recognize in Jesus the potent herald of God's kingdom means Jesus' future words and deeds will only increase confu-

sion about him (verse 25). We have had an example of
that already in scribes and family (3:20–35).

STUDY QUESTIONS: Do these verses suggest that parables are told in order to confuse
people, or to increase their understanding of their own situation?
How do they accomplish that purpose?

4:26–34
Two more parables, and some closing remarks

26   He also said, "This is what the kingdom of
27 God is like. A man throws seed on the land. ·Night
and day, while he sleeps, when he is awake, the
seed is sprouting and growing; how, he does not
28 know. ·Of its own accord the land produces first
the shoot, then the ear, then the full grain in the
29 ear. ·And when the crop is ready, he loses no
time: he starts to reap because the harvest has
come."
30   He also said, "What can we say the kingdom
of God is like? What parable can we find for it?
31 It is like a mustard seed which at the time of its
sowing in the soil is the smallest of all the seeds
32 on earth; ·yet once it is sown it grows into the big-
gest shrub of them all and puts out big branches
so that the birds of the air can shelter in its shade."
33   Using many parables like these, he spoke the
word to them, so far as they were capable of un-
34 derstanding it. ·He would not speak to them except in parables, but he explained everything to
his disciples when they were alone.

✠

Mark returns in these verses to two final parables about seeds, which, along with the parable of the sower, he means us to understand as examples of the many other parables Jesus told (verse 33a). God's kingdom is so new, and its coming so unexpected, that it cannot be described directly, but only in word pictures. Only in that way can we gain some understanding of it (verse 33b). Yet we must remember that these are parables. Their purpose is to illumine the listener's situation. People in the early church may have seen similarities here to their own situation. Verses 27–28 may have been seen as encouragement in the time of waiting between Jesus' resurrection and his return. Despite God's seeming inactivity, the kingdom will come. Verse 32 may have been seen as a reference to the universality of the church's mission. All peoples find "shelter" in the church. But such allegorical elements are foreign to the true parable.

All three parables in Mark make it clear, each in a different way, that if one judges by present appearances —the ordinary activity of the sower, the routine activity of the farmer while his crop grows, the tiny size of the mustard seed—the results will prove one wrong. From the ordinary activity of the sower a great harvest results. From the ordinary routine of the farmer's life a harvest surely results. From the tiny mustard seed a great bush results.

The parables thus shed light on the situation of one who observes Jesus' activities. In facing Jesus, one does not confront an ordinary person, and thus one is not in an ordinary situation, however much it may appear to the contrary. Normal explanations (e.g., 3:21–22) are false when applied to Jesus. Those who persist in them will be proved wrong.

Verses 33–34 summarize Mark's view of the purpose of parables. Only by them can people be shaken loose from an ordinary way of viewing the words and deeds of Jesus, which prelude the coming of God's kingdom. That is why Jesus told parables, in order to provide his listeners a new perspective from which to view their situation vis-à-vis Jesus. Only by recognizing Jesus as the potent herald of God's coming kingdom will one understand one's present situation correctly. Only disciples can understand that!

STUDY QUESTION: Can parables still say something to us who recognize Jesus' relation to God's kingdom, or can we safely ignore their call to see our situation in extraordinary terms?

Mark 4:35 to 5:43
HE DID WONDROUS THINGS

4:35–41
Master of wind and sea

35 With the coming of evening that same day, he said to them, "Let us cross over to the other side."
36 And leaving the crowd behind they took him, just as he was, in the boat; and there were other boats
37 with him. ·Then it began to blow a gale and the waves were breaking into the boat so that it was
38 almost swamped. ·But he was in the stern, his
39 head on the cushion, asleep. ·They woke him and said to him, "Master, do you not care? We are going down!" And he woke up and rebuked the wind and said to the sea, "Quiet now! Be calm!" And the wind dropped, and all was calm again.
40 Then he said to them, "Why are you so fright-
41 ened? How is it that you have no faith?" ·They were filled with awe and said to one another, "Who can this be? Even the wind and the sea obey him."

✠

With this account Mark begins a series of miracle stories that may already have been collected before he received them. Although the reference to Jesus being in the boat ("just as he was, in the boat," verse 36) connects the story to 4:1, a detail forgotten in the rest of

chapter 4 (cf. verse 10), the reference to "other boats
with him" suggests an earlier context, since we hear no
more about these "other boats."

Although this narrative is told in the common form
of Hellenistic miracle stories, it has dimensions that
point beyond an ordinary miracle account. Words used
in verse 39 ("rebuked," "quiet now") are the same
words in the Greek as those used in 1:25 in the story
of the expulsion of a devil ("said sharply," "be
quiet"). This hint of devilish power behind the storm
points the reader to elements of the Old Testament
story of creation. In common with other ancient Near
Eastern peoples, the Israelites knew a story which pictured creation as a battle between God and a sea mon-
ster. Creation resulted when God subdued this mon-
ster (see Jb 9:8, 13; Ps 74:13–14; 89:10; Is
51:9–10; "Rahab" and "Leviathan" are names for it)
and forced the chaotic waters to remain within their
allotted bounds (see Jb 38:8–11; Ps 33:7; 104:9; Pr
8:29). Behind our miracle story there lurks therefore
the awareness that only God has power to order and
sustain his creation. The disciples' final question shows
that, despite their lack of confidence in Jesus' care for
them (verse 39a; their lack of faith, verse 40), they
recognize this point—namely, that Jesus here does what
the Old Testament knew God alone could do (see Ps
89:9; 107:28–29). God's power is now at work in
Jesus.

STUDY QUESTION: Is it still important for us that Jesus
                acted with God's power, or is this
                just an irrelevant, if interesting,
                story?

5:1–20
Jesus heals a demoniac in Gerasa

1,2 5 They reached the country of the Gerasenes on the other side of the lake, ·and no sooner had he left the boat than a man with an unclean
3 spirit came out from the tombs toward him. ·The man lived in the tombs and no one could secure
4 him any more, even with a chain; ·because he had often been secured with fetters and chains but had snapped the chains and broken the fetters,
5 and no one had the strength to control him. ·All night and all day, among the tombs and in the mountains, he would howl and gash himself with
6 stones. ·Catching sight of Jesus from a distance,
7 he ran up and fell at his feet ·and shouted at the top of his voice, "What do you want with me, Jesus, son of the Most High God? Swear by God
8 you will not torture me!"·—For Jesus had been saying to him, "Come out of the man, unclean
9 spirit." ·"What is your name?" Jesus asked. "My name is legion," he answered, "for there are
10 many of us." ·And he begged him earnestly not
11 to send them out of the district. ·Now there was there on the mountainside a great herd of pigs
12 feeding, ·and the unclean spirits begged him,
13 "Send us to the pigs, let us go into them." ·So he gave them leave. With that, the unclean spirits came out and went into the pigs, and the herd of about two thousand pigs charged down the cliff
14 into the lake, and there they were drowned. ·The swineherds ran off and told their story in the town and in the country round about; and the people came to see what had really happened.
15 They came to Jesus and saw the demoniac sitting

there, clothed and in his full senses—the very man
who had had the legion in him before—and they
16 were afraid. ·And those who had witnessed it reported what had happened to the demoniac and
17 what had become of the pigs. ·Then they began
18 to implore Jesus to leave the neighborhood. ·As
he was getting into the boat, the man who had
been possessed begged to be allowed to stay with
19 him. ·Jesus would not let him but said to him,
"Go home to your people and tell them all that
20 the Lord in his mercy has done for you." ·So the
man went off and proceeded to spread throughout the Decapolis all that Jesus had done for him.
And everyone was amazed.

✠

The present shape of this story attests to the many
changes it underwent as it was told and retold in the
primitive church. As details were added to the story,
they did not always fit the narrative precisely, and they
resulted in a rather long, rambling narrative. The attempts to bind and control the demoniac are told twice
over (verses 3, 4), his meeting with Jesus is described
twice (verses 2, 6), we are told twice how people found
out about these events (verses 14, 16), the response to
Jesus' command to the demon to leave (verse 7) comes
before the command is mentioned (verse 8), the demons are not sure if they are one (verse 8) or many
(verses 9, 10, 12), and the details about the herd of
pigs really are not essential to the story (verses
11–13). All of this is evidence of the interest this story
generated, and the additional details it attracted as it
was told and retold.

Yet from this story one point emerges with clarity,
namely the great, even incontestable power Jesus had

at his command. Jesus was confronted with a demoniac
so powerful no one had yet found a way to control him
(verses 3–5). The unclean spirit(s) are so powerful
they are able to resist Jesus' initial command to go out
from the man (verse 8), yet they are reduced to begging to be allowed to inhabit pigs, where once they had
inhabited a man (verses 10–13). The demon(s) know
Jesus' identity (verse 7) and use a common formula
designed to gain control over another person ("swear
by God . . . ," verse 7), both indications for Jesus'
contemporaries that the one uttering such words had
control over his opponent. Yet despite that, Jesus forced
the demons to name themselves, and then, unaffected by
the demons' initial advantage, overcame them. Even
the inordinately large number of pigs in the herd (two
thousand, verse 13) attests to the enormous number of
devils in combat with Jesus; the implication seems to be
that only such a large number of pigs would be
sufficient to provide the devils a new dwelling place.

There is another point made in this story which we
have already found in Mark (e.g., in 3:22)—namely,
that miracles as such do not lead to faith in Jesus. In
this story, the reaction to the curing of the demoniac is
not faith in Jesus but fear (verse 15) and the desire to
be rid of him (verse 17). The early Christians who told
and retold the story did not associate this reaction with
the economic hardship caused by the loss of so many
swine. Rather, the point clearly is that seeing miracles
of Jesus, even being convinced he could do them, as
these people clearly were, is not enough to awaken
faith in Jesus. Such faith, Mark knew, is possible only
after cross and resurrection. These stories can be understood in the light of that final fate of Jesus (which is

why Mark put them into a longer narrative that climaxed in cross and resurrection). Prior to Jesus' final
fate, events like this only awakened fear and mistrust.

The story ends with another surprise. Instead of
a command to keep silent about this event (cf. 1:34, 44;
3:12), the demoniac is told to spread news of it
(the Decapolis [verse 20] was a region of ten cities under direct Roman rule to the east and south of the Sea of
Galilee). Further, instead of being asked to give up
family and friends for Jesus (cf. 10:29–30), this man is
forbidden to accompany Jesus and is told to return to
his own people (verse 19). There is apparently no set
formula for discipleship. In each instance, the circumstances determine what is appropriate for one who
wants to obey Jesus.

This story was told, therefore, to make theological
points, not to satisfy our historical curiosity. Even the
location is wrong for that, since Gerasa is located thirty
miles from the shore of the Sea of Galilee. The story
does not intend to make us wonder about the pigs, or
try to determine what may have excited them to their
destruction, nor to wonder how so many demons could
inhabit one human being.

Rather, this story, like the one before it, was intended to show the incontestable power by which Jesus
spoke and acted during his earthly career. It was to
make that point that the many details were added to
the story from time to time, and it is that point that still
stands out for those who read it with eyes to see what
Mark wants to tell us. In Jesus, God's own power is at
work among his people—Jew and, here, gentile alike.
Therefore his words about God's coming kingdom *must*
be taken with utmost seriousness.

STUDY QUESTION: Are there any evidences in our day
that Jesus continues to use such
power for his people?

5:21–43
Jesus is master over sickness and death

21 When Jesus had crossed again in the boat to
the other side, a large crowd gathered around him
22 and he stayed by the lakeside. ·Then one of the
synagogue officials came up, Jairus by name, and
23 seeing him, fell at his feet ·and pleaded with him
earnestly, saying, "My little daughter is desperately sick. Do come and lay your hands on her
24 to make her better and save her life." ·Jesus went
with him and a large crowd followed him; they
were pressing all around him.
25 Now there was a woman who had suffered
26 from a hemorrhage for twelve years; ·after long
and painful treatment under various doctors, she
had spent all she had without being any the better
27 for it, in fact, she was getting worse. ·She had
heard about Jesus, and she came up behind him
28 through the crowd and touched his cloak. ·"If I
can touch even his clothes," she had told herself,
29 "I shall be well again." ·And the source of the
bleeding dried up instantly, and she felt in her-
30 self that she was cured of her complaint. ·Imme-
diately aware that power had gone out from him,
Jesus turned around in the crowd and said, "Who
31 touched my clothes?" ·His disciples said to him,
"You see how the crowd is pressing around you
32 and yet you say, 'Who touched me?'" ·But he
continued to look all around to see who had done
33 it. ·Then the woman came forward, frightened

and trembling because she knew what had happened to her, and she fell at his feet and told him
34 the whole truth. ·"My daughter," he said, "your faith has restored you to health; go in peace and be free from your complaint."
35 While he was still speaking some people arrived from the house of the synagogue official to say, "Your daughter is dead: why put the Master to
36 any further trouble?" ·But Jesus had overheard this remark of theirs and he said to the official,
37 "Do not be afraid; only have faith." ·And he allowed no one to go with him except Peter and
38 James and John the brother of James. ·So they came to the official's house and Jesus noticed all the commotion, with people weeping and wailing
39 unrestrainedly. ·He went in and said to them, "Why all this commotion and crying? The child
40 is not dead, but asleep." ·But they laughed at him. So he turned them all out and, taking with him the child's father and mother and his own companions, he went into the place where the child
41 lay. ·And taking the child by the hand he said to her, "Talitha, kum!" which means, "Little girl, I
42 tell you to get up." ·The little girl got up at once and began to walk about, for she was twelve years old. At this they were overcome with astonish-
43 ment, ·and he ordered them strictly not to let anyone know about it, and told them to give her something to eat.

✠

This is the third account that demonstrates Jesus' lordship: over nature (4:35–41), over demons (5:1–20), and over sickness and death (5:21–43). Two stories are sandwiched together here. A careful study of their style reveals differences significant enough to allow us to conclude they were composed independently of one another. Various similarities of detail

probably account for their association with one another. Both tell about females helped, both concern situations of desperate nature, both use the number
twelve (the duration of the woman's sickness, the little
girl's age), and, perhaps most importantly, both stories
tell of faith in connection with healings. We cannot rule
out the possibility that they were already associated in
Mark's source, but his fondness for inserting one story
into another (e.g., 11:12–25; cf. also 3:20–35;
6:7–32) makes it likely he is responsible for their present combination. Normally, when two accounts are
put together like this, one comments in some way on
the other. In this instance, perhaps the story of the
healing of the woman gains in seriousness by its association with a story in which someone is raised from the
dead.

The story of the woman contains a description of the
incurable nature of her affliction (verses 25–26). That
makes her cure all the more remarkable, and is a common emphasis in secular miracle stories of this time.
Nor is the flow of healing power from someone's clothing unique to this account (cf. Ac 19:11–12). What is
important here is that the desire to touch Jesus' garments in full expectation of healing (verse 28) is
identified as faith. Indeed, it is that faith rather than the
touch alone that has restored her to health (verse 34).
That Jesus could perceive her touch in the midst of a
jostling crowd (verses 30–31) shows that her intention
in touching him made her touch unique. Faith seems to
mean here, as it did in 2:4–5, letting nothing hinder
one from seeking out Jesus' help.

Perhaps most remarkable of all, however, one of the
terms used for healing in this story is not the usual one
but is a word having the basic meaning "to save." In

verse 28, the woman says to herself, "If I can touch
him, I will be saved," and verse 34 can similarly be
translated, "Your faith has saved you." That meaning
is reinforced in verse 34 by Jesus' use of the word
"peace," which has clear overtones, in its Old Testament use, of salvation as wholeness and restoration.
Further, when Jesus addresses the woman as "daughter," he includes her in the messianic family of those
who find in Jesus their way to God (cf. 3:33–35).
There is therefore reflected in this story of a hemorrhage stanched the clear indication that faithful expect-
ancy of God's help in Jesus brings one into the orbit of
salvation.

Reflections of a deeper meaning are also present in
the story of the little girl raised from the dead. Her
death has put her beyond Jesus' power to help; so at
least the messengers think. Jesus' response reveals the
deeper dimension in this story. The phrase "Do not be
afraid" is a regular formula used when God appears (a
"theophanic formula"; see Gn 15:1; 21:17; 26:24;
46:3; Jg 6:23; Dn 10:12, 19). The verse is thus more
than encouragement to a saddened father. It gives the
clue about who this Jesus really is.

That the girl is dead is shown by the presence of
mourners, customarily hired to lament the dead. Jesus'
words about sleep, therefore, in verse 39 do not constitute a medical diagnosis. They are the confident assertion by one who acts with God's power that death itself
cannot thwart him. With a touch and a word, the sovereign Jesus restores life to the dead girl.

Both stories are told in a form familiar to Mark's
Hellenistic contemporaries. The desperate nature of the
malady, the effectiveness of the cure, and the inclusion
of a phrase in a foreign tongue (verse 41) all belong to

the usual miracle story. The unique point of our narratives is thus not to be sought in such details. Rather those elements which go beyond an interest in a miracle as such reveal to us the point Mark sought to make by using these stories.

Such elements in these stories tell of one who worked by God's own power, and who, by awakening faith in those who heard of him and then sought him out (verses 22, 27), bestowed on them the gifts of God's own salvation, namely wholeness and life. Yet those elements tell us even more. Who would not see Jesus' own resurrection prefigured, however dimly, in the command to the little girl to arise (the same word is used in the New Testament to refer to Jesus' resurrection)? The stories thus contain hints, for those with eyes to see them, about who this Jesus is. He can pronounce God's salvation (verse 34), he can use the theophanic formula that announces God's presence (verse 36), he can wield God's sovereign power over death itself, as he will one day become the one by whom death is conquered for all humanity.

The hints remain veiled, however, for us who read the stories as for those who saw and heard Jesus. It was still all too possible to see in him simply a worker of wonders, in total disregard of his own announced connection to God's coming kingdom. Until cross and empty tomb, that possibility of misconstruing Jesus remains. Indeed, it predominates even among the disciples who in the end forsook him and fled. For that reason, Mark pictures Jesus as insisting that information about his wondrous deeds not be spread abroad (verse 43a). That insistence is theologically, not historically, motivated. Too many people knew the little girl had died to keep her resurrection a secret for long.

Rather, such insistences point to Mark's awareness that only in light of cross and resurrection can Jesus finally and fully be understood.

STUDY QUESTION: What other hints can you find in Mark that point to his belief that only the cross and resurrection reveal the true meaning of Jesus?

Mark 6:1–6
THE CROSS FORESHADOWED:
JESUS IS REJECTED BY HIS OWN

¹ 6 Going from that district, he went to his home town and his disciples accompanied ² him. ·With the coming of the sabbath he began teaching in the synagogue and most of them were astonished when they heard him. They said, "Where did the man get all this? What is this wisdom that has been granted him, and these mira- ³ cles that are worked through him? ·This is the carpenter, surely, the son of Mary, the brother of James and Joset and Jude and Simon? His sisters, too, are they not here with us?" And they would ⁴ not accept him. ·And Jesus said to them, "A prophet is only despised in his own country, among his own relations and in his own house"; ⁵ and he could work no miracle there, though he cured a few sick people by laying his hands on ⁶ them. ·He was amazed at their lack of faith.

✠

In stark contrast to the triumphant lordship displayed in the preceding accounts (4:35 to 5:43), Jesus is here ridiculed and rejected in his own home town. The place Mark put this story and the part he played in shaping it (shown by Markan vocabulary and style) show that he intended that contrast.

Contrary to normal Jewish practice, Jesus is identified by his mother rather than his father, although

some manuscripts read "son of the carpenter and
Mary." Yet Mark nowhere in his Gospel mentions Joseph, perhaps because he had long since died, perhaps
because Jesus' true father is God. Later church disputes
over whether Mary remained a virgin after Jesus' birth
raised problems about how "brothers" and "sisters"
are to be understood here. In Mark's context, their
mention is merely intended to show that the villagers
perceived Jesus as no different from any of them. His
family was known, including his brothers and sisters.
The problem of Mary's virginity is simply absent from
Mark's Gospel.

The point of this passage is not the nature of Jesus'
family relationships, however. It is his rejection by his
own people. Incredible though it may be, it is surely intended by Mark to foreshadow the ultimate fate Jesus
will experience at the hands of "his own people"—i.e.,
disciples, Jews, indeed, all humanity.

Verse 5 does not mean that miracles are possible
only where faith is present; some are accomplished despite faith's absence (e.g., in 4:35–41). Yet it does
show that, for Mark, the meaning of Jesus' miracles is
not grasped except through faith in him. Awe at Jesus
the wonder-worker is an inadequate reaction for Mark.
Only faith-filled following will do.

STUDY QUESTIONS: Can you find other places in this
Gospel where Mark hints at Jesus'
final rejection by "his own"? If we
understand "his own" as those
who ought to know him best, is
such rejection still a problem?

Jesus Begins His Final Journey:
Mission and Miracles
Mark 6:7 to 8:21

Mark 6:7–29
JOURNEY FOR MISSION AND
THE DEATH OF JOHN

6:7–13
The Twelve sent out on mission

He made a tour around the villages, teaching.
7 Then he summoned the Twelve and began to send
them out in pairs giving them authority over the
8 unclean spirits. ·And he instructed them to take
nothing for the journey except a staff—no bread,
9 no haversack, no coppers for their purses. ·They
were to wear sandals but, he added, "Do not take
10 a spare tunic." ·And he said to them, "If you enter a house anywhere, stay there until you leave
11 the district. ·And if any place does not welcome
you and people refuse to listen to you, as you
walk away shake off the dust from under your feet
12 as a sign to them." ·So they set off to preach re-
13 pentance; ·and they cast out many devils, and
anointed many sick people with oil and cured
them.

✠

With this story—shaped again in large part by Mark,
as style and vocabulary show—a new segment of the
Gospel begins, which will end (in 8:11–21), as did the
first two segments, with Jesus misunderstood (cf.

3:1–6 and 6:1–6). Similarly, as the second segment began with stories that implied Jesus responded to rejection with the choice of twelve to "be with him" and to engage in missionary activity (3:7–19), so this third segment begins with an account of Jesus sending out the Twelve on a mission to preach and heal, on the heels of Jesus' rejection in his home town. Since in each case the segment begins with a story displaying signs of Markan literary activity, it is clear that this repeated pattern reflects Mark's own design. Perhaps it was meant as encouragement for later missionaries who suffer similar rejections.

The instructions to the Twelve (verses 8–9) probably indicate they are to rely on God for all their needs. Missionaries who provide against every anticipated adversity (money, extra clothing, and the like) are scarcely believable when they announce the nearness of God's kingdom. The authority to cast out devils (or unclean spirits—they are the same) shows that God's victory over Satan, already visible in Jesus, continues in the activity of those Jesus sends out.

The missionaries are not to move from house to house seeking better accommodations (verse 10), and when they do meet refusal, they are to symbolize God's judgment against such an act by separating themselves completely from that region, even to being rid of the dust that clings to their sandals.

STUDY QUESTION: Are there any activities of modern missionaries, here or abroad, which render unbelievable their message of God's forgiving love in Christ?

6:14–29
The cross foreshadowed:
Herod and John the Baptist

14 Meanwhile King Herod had heard about him, since by now his name was well-known. Some were saying, "John the Baptist has risen from the dead, and that is why miraculous powers are at
15 work in him." ·Others said, "He is Elijah"; others again, "He is a prophet, like the prophets we used
16 to have." ·But when Herod heard this he said, "It is John whose head I cut off; he has risen from the dead."

17 Now it was this same Herod who had sent to have John arrested, and had him chained up in prison because of Herodias, his brother Philip's
18 wife whom he had married. ·For John had told Herod, "It is against the law for you to have your
19 brother's wife." ·As for Herodias, she was furious with him and wanted to kill him; but she was not
20 able to, ·because Herod was afraid of John, knowing him to be a good and holy man, and gave him his protection. When he had heard him speak he was greatly perplexed, and yet he liked to listen to him.

21 An opportunity came on Herod's birthday when he gave a banquet for the nobles of his court, for his army officers and for the leading figures in
22 Galilee. ·When the daughter of this same Herodias came in and danced, she delighted Herod and his guests; so the king said to the girl, "Ask me anything you like and I will give it you."
23 And he swore her an oath, "I will give you any-
24 thing you ask, even half my kingdom." ·She went out and said to her mother, "What shall I ask for?"

25 She replied, "The head of John the Baptist." ·The
girl hurried straight back to the king and made her
request, "I want you to give me John the Baptist's
26 head, here and now, on a dish." ·The king was
deeply distressed but, thinking of the oaths he
had sworn and of his guests, he was reluctant to
27 break his word to her. ·So the king at once sent
one of the bodyguard with orders to bring John's
28 head. ·The man went off and beheaded him in
prison; then he brought the head on a dish and
gave it to the girl, and the girl gave it to her
29 mother. ·When John's disciples heard about this,
they came and took his body and laid it in a tomb.

✠

This story, set between the sending out of the Twelve
(6:7) and their return (6:30), is a rather fanciful account of the fate of John the Baptist, told long after the
fact (John's arrest came before Jesus began his public
ministry, according to Mark; see 1:14), with the apparent purpose of displaying John as the forerunner of
Jesus not only by what he said but also by the fate he
suffered. We have here intimations that when Jesus left
his home town, he began the journey that would end
with the cross.

The attempts to explain who Jesus was (verses
14–16) show that the impression Jesus made was as a
wonder-worker. They also show the variety of interpretations possible to account for such a person. While
Elijah was expected to return before the last days (see
Ml 3:23 [= 4:5]; Si 48:4–11), he was also famous
for his miracles (see 1 K 17:10–24). Herod's memory
of John's death (verse 16) gives Mark the narrative
opportunity to include a tale about that event.

The account of John's beheading, written prior to

Mark as its language and style show, is characterized more by its lurid detail than by its historical reliability. Herod was a tetrarch, not a king, who ruled at the pleasure of Rome; he could not give up an acre without Rome's permission (see verses 22–23). A girl of Salome's social standing would not have provided entertainment as a dancing girl at the kind of party Herod gave (verses 21–22). And the reference to Herodias as "his brother Philip's wife" (verse 17) is ambiguous at best, since Herod had two brothers who bore that name, Philip the Tetrarch, and Herod Philip.

The enmity between Herodias and John the Baptist is confirmed by another contemporary writer, however. Herod did in fact divorce his wife, a Nabatean princess, to marry Herodias, and John denounced that action. The father of the Nabatean princess later avenged that dishonor by crushing Herod's army, and would have overrun his territory had not Rome intervened to restore the balance of power.

The account in Mark thus has a historical basis, but it has been filled out with a variety of details. While some of those details seem little more than gossip, others have a more serious intent. Some influence on the story seems to have come from accounts in 1 Kings 18 and 19 (cf. especially 19:1–2) of the hostility between Jezebel and Elijah. Since John will later be identified as the returned Elijah (Mk 9:13), such influence accords with Mark's understanding of John. Perhaps most importantly of all, this story gives us a hint of Jesus' own fate. He, like John, will be put to death with the conspiratorial connivance of prominent people. It was probably for that reason that Mark found a place for this strange story, the only one in his Gospel in which Jesus plays no part at all. John, the

promised Elijah who was to herald the last times, is
forerunner to Jesus in his manner of death as well as in
his message.

STUDY QUESTIONS: Are there modern attempts to
come to terms with Jesus, similar
to those we find in verses 14–16?
Why are there so many different
attempts to explain him?

MIGHTY ACTS AND MANY ARGUMENTS

6:30–44
Jesus feeds many with little

³⁰ The apostles rejoined Jesus and told him all ³¹ they had done and taught. ·Then he said to them, "You must come away to some lonely place all by yourselves and rest for a while"; for there were so many coming and going that the apostles had no ³² time even to eat. ·So they went off in a boat to a lonely place where they could be by themselves. ³³ But people saw them going, and many could guess where; and from every town they all hurried to ³⁴ the place on foot and reached it before them. ·So as he stepped ashore he saw a large crowd; and he took pity on them because they were like sheep without a shepherd, and he set himself to teach ³⁵ them at some length. ·By now it was getting very late, and his disciples came up to him and said, "This is a lonely place and it is getting very late, ³⁶ so send them away, and they can go to the farms and villages round about, to buy themselves some- ³⁷ thing to eat." ·He replied, "Give them something to eat yourselves." They answered, "Are we to go and spend two hundred denarii on bread for them ³⁸ to eat?" ·"How many loaves have you?" he asked. "Go and see." And when they had found out they ³⁹ said, "Five, and two fish." ·Then he ordered them to get all the people together in groups on the ⁴⁰ green grass, ·and they sat down on the ground in

41 squares of hundreds and fifties. ·Then he took the
five loaves and the two fish, raised his eyes to
heaven and said the blessing; then he broke the
loaves and handed them to his disciples to distribute among the people. He also shared out the
42 two fish among them all. ·They all ate as much as
43 they wanted. ·They collected twelve basketfuls of
44 scraps and pieces of fish. ·Those who had eaten the
loaves numbered five thousand men.

✠

These verses present quite clearly a story cast in the
traditional miracle form (verses 35–44), with an introduction provided by Mark to fit it into its present context (verses 30–33). Many of the details are thus dic-
tated by the form of the story, rather than because of
any theological intention (e.g., the disciples distribute
the food, verse 41, because the crowd is so great, not as
intentional prefigurement of the later services of the
diaconate).

The story of the return of the disciples from their
mission bears enough signs of Markan composition to
allow us to conclude that he is responsible for its present form, even if there is some tradition underlying it.
We learn nothing of the missionary journey, save that it
was completed in accordance with instructions (cf.
verse 30 with verses 7, 12–13).

The phrase that begins verse 34 (Greek: "And when
he came out, he saw . . .") is more appropriate for
coming out of a house (see the same word used in
1:29, 35; 2:13), indicating an earlier context for this
story in Mark's source. As verse 36 shows, a totally
deserted area is not envisioned by the story. There are
farms and villages where food would be available. The

problem, similarly, in verse 37 is lack of enough money
to buy sufficient bread, not the unavailability of any
bread in that location. When a deserted area is envisioned, as in 8:1–10, such details are changed (see especially 8:3–4). Mark is therefore the one responsible
for locating this story, in his introduction, in a place
where Jesus and the Twelve would be free from crowds
(verse 31). Nevertheless, Jesus cannot escape those
crowds, again a typical Markan motif (cf. 2:13; 3:7).

Because the story of the feeding is cast in miracle
form, there is no foundation for the notion that it was
originally intended simply to tell of the way Jesus' loving spirit induced a great crowd of people to share food
with one another. The emphasis on the enormity of the
problem (verses 35–38; no food, insufficient money,
insignificant resources in only five loaves and two fish)
and the details intended to prove a miracle had occurred (verses 42–44; all had enough, with a large
amount left over; the great number fed) make it clear
that from its inception this story was intended to tell of
a wondrous deed of Jesus.

The story is, however, evocative of other events told
in the Bible: the children of Israel fed with manna in
the wilderness (Ex 16), Elijah feeding men with few
provisions (2 K 4:42–44; Jn 6:9 makes such an evoca-
tion explicit with mention of "barley loaves"), even the
institution of the Eucharist (cf. verse 41 with 14:22).
Yet later references to this story by Mark (6:52;
8:17–21) make it clear that he saw it as an example of
the inability of the disciples to understand Jesus, even
on the basis of as spectacular an act as this. If the reference to the Eucharist was intentional in the pre-
Markan tradition of this story, Mark may deliberately
have tried to disassociate the two, since for him the Eu-

charist is based not on Jesus' miraculous deeds but
rather on his sacrifice on the cross, as the account of
the words of institution makes clear (cf. 14:22–25 with
the context of 14:17–31, and indeed, the passion account as a whole). Perhaps Mark wants to emphasize
that Jesus cannot be understood apart from the cross,
even when the disciples share in an event that so clearly
points to who Jesus is: like Elijah, he can feed multi-
tudes from little. Indeed, like God himself, he can provide food in the wilderness.

STUDY QUESTION: Why do you think Mark wanted to
emphasize so strongly that one can-
not rightly understand Jesus until
one knows he was crucified and
risen?

6:45–52
Jesus walks a stormy sea

45 Directly after this he made his disciples get into
the boat and go on ahead to Bethsaida, while he
46 himself sent the crowd away. ·After saying good-
by to them he went off into the hills to pray.
47 When evening came, the boat was far out on the
48 lake, and he was alone on the land. ·He could see
they were worn out with rowing, for the wind was
against them; and about the fourth watch of the
night he came toward them, walking on the lake.
49 He was going to pass them by, ·but when they saw
him walking on the lake they thought it was a
50 ghost and cried out; ·for they had all seen him and
were terrified. But he at once spoke to them, and

⁵¹ said, "Courage! It is I! Do not be afraid." ·Then he got into the boat with them, and the wind dropped. They were utterly and completely dum-
⁵² founded, ·because they had not seen what the miracle of the loaves meant; their minds were closed.

✠

By any measure, this is a perplexing story. A number of details within the narrative stand in tension to one another, and to the larger context in which the narrative is found. There are two reasons given for dismissing the disciples: to permit Jesus to send away the crowd (verse 45), and to give Jesus solitude to pray (verse 46). Again, though Jesus sees the boat in difficulty "when evening came" (verse 47), he does not go to them until the "fourth watch"—i.e., between 3:00 and 6:00 A.M. And when he does reach them, it is not to help after all; he "was going to pass them by" (verse 48). Again, Jesus compels the disciples to set sail for a destination (Bethsaida, verse 45) which they do not reach (see verse 53); the dismissal and the disciples' trip "far out on the lake" take place before evening came, yet in verse 35 it was already "very late."

Such narrative problems make it clear that Mark put this story here, and adapted it to this context (verses 45 and 52 almost surely are due to Mark), for reasons other than a desire to give us accurate historical or geographical information. If, as seems very likely, Mark appended verse 52, that will give the reason why he included the story here. The reason is that the disciples were still totally unable to understand Jesus, even after he fed a multitude with little and walked on the sea. (In the Old Testament, the act of walking on the sea is

attributed to God—Jb 9:8; Ps 77:19; Is 43:16. Greco-
Roman authors also regularly attributed it to various
gods and heroes.) Had they perceived the meaning of
Jesus (i.e., his divine status and mission) from the
feeding, Mark implies, their terror (verse 50) and confusion (verse 51) would not have occurred. Yet their
inability to understand seems beyond their control. The
language of verse 52 clearly implies that.

What the story may originally have meant—a mani-
festation of Jesus' true status, comparable to the
transfiguration; a stormy sea calmed, comparable to the
story in 4:35–41—can only be speculated. What it
means here in Mark's context seems clear enough. Seeing the miraculous power Jesus manifested during his
earthly career is not enough to enable one to understand him. In Mark's view, such understanding awaits a
final event: the cross.

STUDY QUESTION: What value does a story like this
still have for us, who know about
the cross and can thus, in part at
least, understand Jesus?

6:53–56
People flock to Jesus

53   Having made the crossing, they came to land at
54   Gennesaret and tied up. ·No sooner had they
stepped out of the boat than people recognized
55   him, ·and started hurrying all through the coun-
tryside and brought the sick on stretchers to wher-

⁵⁶ ever they heard he was. ·And wherever he went,
to village, or town, or farm, they laid down the
sick in the open spaces, begging him to let them
touch even the fringe of his cloak. And all those
who touched him were cured.

✠

Although language and style indicate Mark had a
hand in shaping these verses, the reference to the land-
ing at Gennesaret, contrary to Jesus' instruction in
verse 45, and to the fringes on Jesus' garment (cf. Nb
15:38–39; Mark nowhere else mentions such details)
point to underlying tradition. Attempts to account for
the change in destination (e.g., suggesting that perhaps
they were blown off course by wind, or that Jesus
changed instructions after getting into the boat) remain
pure speculation and add nothing to our understanding
of Mark.

The point made in these verses is common enough in
Mark. Crowds press in on Jesus (cf. 3:7–8, 20; 4:1;
5:21), frequently to take advantage of his healing
powers (1:32; 3:10). Verse 56 indicates that the
woman healed by touching Jesus' garment (5:27–28)
was not unique. In fact, these summaries seem intent
on saying that the narratives of healing Mark recites
are simply examples of an activity repeated many times
over.

The contrast between the attitude of these people toward Jesus and that of the religious leaders in the following story is striking and may account for this summary being placed here. Common people flock to Jesus
to be healed (the verb can also mean "to be saved").
Pharisees and scribes pick at any point they can find to
discredit and reject him (7:1–2).

STUDY QUESTION: How do you account for the difference between these people, who seek Jesus out because of his miracles, and the disciples, who were "dumfounded" by a miracle (verse 51)?

7:1–13
Good rules and bad results

¹ 7 The Pharisees and some of the scribes who had come from Jerusalem gathered around him, ² and they noticed that some of his disciples were eating with unclean hands, that is, without washing ³ them. ·For the Pharisees, and the Jews in general, follow the tradition of the elders and never eat without washing their arms as far as the elbow; ⁴ and on returning from the market place they never eat without first sprinkling themselves. There are also many other observances which have been handed down to them concerning the wash- ⁵ ing of cups and pots and bronze dishes. ·So these Pharisees and scribes asked him, "Why do your disciples not respect the tradition of the elders ⁶ but eat their food with unclean hands?" ·He answered, "It was of you hypocrites that Isaiah so rightly prophesied in this passage of scripture:

This people honors me only with lip-service,
while their hearts are far from me.
⁷ The worship they offer me is worthless,
the doctrines they teach are only human regulations.

⁸ You put aside the commandment of God to cling ⁹ to human traditions." ·And he said to them, "How

ingeniously you get around the commandment of
10 God in order to preserve your own tradition! ·For
Moses said: Do your duty to your father and your
mother, and, Anyone who curses father or
11 mother must be put to death. ·But you say, 'If a
man says to his father or mother: Anything I have
that I might have used to help you is Corban
12 (that is, dedicated to God), ·then he is forbidden
from that moment to do anything for his father or
13 mother.' ·In this way you make God's word null
and void for the sake of your tradition which you
have handed down. And you do many other things
like this."

☧

There are indications that Mark assembled this passage from individual traditions he knew from his
sources. Verses 3–4 interrupt the sentence in which
they occur (verses 2–5; the English has smoothed the
rougher Greek text), and seem to be an explanation
Mark inserted. The phrase introducing verse 9 is often
used by Mark when he connects independent traditions.
The repetition of the point in verses 8 and 9 may be the
reason Mark felt it appropriate to connect them.

This is the last incident Mark reports of Jesus' Galilean ministry. Perhaps he chose these passages to show
the kind of mounting opposition Jesus faced in Galilee
because of the activity of religious leaders "from Jerusalem" (verse 1). It was that opposition that brought
his Galilean ministry to an end, as it would be instru-
mental in bringing his career to an end, on a cross in
Jerusalem.

At issue is not hygienic but ritual purity (cf. Lv
22:1–16). While verses 3–4 describe acts not univer-
sally observed by Palestinian Jews in Jesus' time, they

may reflect practices of Jews living outside of Palestine in Mark's time. In any case, the problem centers on the "traditions of the elders," or the oral law. These traditions were developed in an attempt to clarify certain provisions of the written law (the Torah—the first five books of the Old Testament), to apply them to changing situations, and to see that major provisions remained unbroken. This latter activity, called "building a fence around the law," set up many lesser regulations designed to protect a major law. For example, if labor is forbidden on the Sabbath (Ex 20:8–11), provisions to forbid carrying any burden or doing any traveling will make sure no labor can be performed.

The question here is thus not so much the validity of the law as it is the validity of the Pharisaic interpretation of the law. This was a problem not only for Jesus but for the early church as well (note that the question concerns Jesus' *disciples*—i.e., his followers—in verses 2 and 5). Verse 6 shows the real issue: hypocrisy. Yet this hypocrisy is not simply personal insincerity. It means here substituting legalisms for obedience to the true intention of the law. Thus, the very sincerity with which the Pharisees follow their religious traditions leads them into the hypocrisy of ignoring the true intention of the law. The Pharisees' problem is not lack of sincere religious zeal. Rather, it is a problem of misdirected religious zeal (cf. Rm 10:2–3) which leads them away from God and his will. The more sincere they were about their traditions, the more they were led by them to oppose God's will, and to oppose Jesus as well.

The example of such "hypocrisy" in verses 10–12 does not reflect official Pharisaic Judaism of any period we know. It may refer to an individual case, or to the practice in some isolated area. The point, however, still stands. Reverence for Pharisaic traditions leads inevitably to opposition to what God really wants (verses 7, 8, 13). This is most clearly illustrated in Pharisaic opposition to Jesus. Their zeal for their understanding of God's will led them to oppose God's own Son. That is the irony and the tragedy of Jewish opposition to Jesus.

STUDY QUESTIONS: Do we run any danger of allowing religious rules to get in the way of our doing God's will? Can the pure intentions of those who make those rules guarantee such a thing won't happen?

7:14–23
What makes a person unacceptable to God?

14 He called the people to him again and said,
15 "Listen to me, all of you, and understand. ·Nothing that goes into a man from outside can make him unclean; it is the things that come out of a
16 man that make him unclean. ·If anyone has ears to hear, let him listen to this."
17 When he had gone back into the house, away from the crowd, his disciples questioned him about
18 the parable. ·He said to them, "Do you not understand either? Can you not see that whatever goes into a man from outside cannot make him un-
19 clean, ·because it does not go into his heart but through his stomach and passes out into the sewer?" (Thus he pronounced all foods clean.)
20 And he went on, "It is what comes out of a man

21 that makes him unclean. ·For it is from within,
   from men's hearts, that evil intentions emerge:
22 fornication, theft, murder, adultery, ·avarice, mal-
   lice, deceit, indecency, envy, slander, pride, folly.
23 All these evil things come from within and make
   a man unclean."

✠

In this continuation of 7:1–13, Jesus turns from remarks about Pharisaic interpretation of the law to an
attack on the basic premise of the whole Jewish legal
code: the difference between clean and unclean foods.
The point of these verses is unmistakable. No food can
render a person unclean—i.e., unacceptable to God.
Consequently, all rules forbidding those who observe
dietary laws to eat with those who do not are also
abrogated. Such a statement is revolutionary, not only
for Jews but for all who by some form of asceticism
think to render themselves acceptable to God. Perhaps
because of its radical nature it is called a "parable"—
i.e., a potentially confusing saying (cf. 3:23)—and is
given further explanation (verses 17–23). As the concluding remark of verse 19 makes clear, however, the
intent of this passage is to abolish all differentiation between foods for religious reasons.

Yet if Jesus stated this as clearly as this passage indicates, it is difficult to imagine how attitudes toward
food could have been so divisive in the primitive
church. There was considerable dispute about it (cf.
Ac 11:2–3; 15:1–2, 5; Ga 2:11–13; Col 2:20–22),
and a compromise solution seems the best that could be
reached (Ac 15:23–29). In light of that, can Jesus
have made statements as clear as those contained in
these verses? Or do these verses reflect a later attempt

by the gentile church to justify its repudiation of Jewish dietary laws (cf. Rm 14:14)?

There is evidence to indicate that these words in their present form may not come directly from Jesus. The signs of Markan composition are unmistakable: the typical transition in verse 14, the exhortation in verse 16 (cf. 4:9, 23), the private instruction of the disciples in verse 17a (cf. 4:10; 9:28; 10:10) and the Markan formulation of 17b (the same language appears in 4:10), the Markan attachment formula in verse 18. Furthermore, the list of vices in verses 21–22 is more characteristic of Hellenistic than of Palestinian Jewish writing, and points to a time later than that of Jesus (for other, similar lists, cf. Rm 1:29–31; Ga 5:19–21a; 1 Tm 1:9–10; 2 Tm 3:2–4).

On the other hand, it was just such a radical attitude toward the Jewish law that got Jesus into trouble with Jewish religious authorities (e.g., 3:1–6) and that provoked precisely those disputes with them which are pictured throughout the gospel traditions. If these words themselves do not go back to Jesus, the sentiment about the Jewish law surely does, and we are justified in finding in them an accurate reflection of the mind of Jesus.

STUDY QUESTIONS: If the distinction between sacred and profane is eliminated in respect to foods but not actions (verses 21–22), are there other aspects of our life where that distinction is to be eliminated? Where it is to be applied?

7:24–30
Can gentiles also come to Jesus?

24   He left that place and set out for the territory
     of Tyre. There he went into a house and did not
     want anyone to know he was there but he could
25   not pass unrecognized. ·A woman whose little
     daughter had an unclean spirit heard about him
26   straightaway and came and fell at his feet. ·Now
     the woman was a pagan, by birth a Syrophoeni-
     cian, and she begged him to cast the devil out of
27   her daughter. ·And he said to her, "The children
     should be fed first, because it is not fair to take the
     children's food and throw it to the house dogs."
28   But she spoke up: "Ah yes, sir," she replied, "but
     the house dogs under the table can eat the chil-
29   dren's scraps." ·And he said to her, "For saying
     this, you may go home happy: the devil has gone
30   out of your daughter." ·So she went off to her
     home and found the child lying on the bed and the
     devil gone.

☩

The occurrence of this story immediately following
the dispute about Jewish legalism contrasts clearly the
reception Jesus found among Jewish religious authorities on the one hand and gentiles on the other. The
point of the story is the dialogue in verses 27–28,
where the woman's persistence in the face of Jesus'
sense of priority (first Jews, only then gentiles, cf. Rm
1:16; 2:9–10; Ac 19:8–9) finds its reward. Her persistence is surely to be understood as faith (Matthew

makes that explicit, Mt 15:28). She is confident Jesus not only can but will help her. Such confidence in Jesus overcomes all barriers of race, a point the later acceptance of the gospel by other gentiles will confirm (see Ac 10:34–35; 15:6–9).

Mark is responsible for giving the story that explicit point, by locating it in the "territory of Tyre" (verse 24). The original locus of the story was probably Galilee. The careful identification of the woman as a Syrophoenician gentile would be more appropriate if that nationality were exceptional (as in Galilee) rather than the rule (as in the area of Syrophoenicia). Indeed, if Jesus was in the region of Tyre, a non-Jewish land, then he himself was not restricting the "food" (gospel) to the "children" (Jews) as he claims is proper (verse 27). By his geographical framing, Mark has made explicit what was already implicit in the story, namely that gentiles who come to Jesus in faith find acceptance. Thus, the possibility of a mission to the gentiles, already implicit in the original story (verses 25–30), was carried a step further by Mark. His point is clear. The later gentile mission can legitimately trace its roots right back to Jesus.

STUDY QUESTION: Does the miracle-story context have any significance, or add any weight, to the point Mark is making by his use of this account?

7:31–37
Jesus heals a deaf-mute

31   Returning from the district of Tyre he went by
      way of Sidon toward the Sea of Galilee, right
32 through the Decapolis region. ·And they brought
      him a deaf man who had an impediment in his
      speech; and they asked him to lay his hand on him.
33 He took him aside in private, away from the
      crowd, put his fingers into the man's ears and
34 touched his tongue with spittle. ·Then looking up
      to heaven he sighed; and he said to him, "Eph-
35 phatha," that is, "Be opened." ·And his ears were
      opened, and the ligament of his tongue was loos-
36 ened and he spoke clearly. ·And Jesus ordered
      them to tell no one about it, but the more he in-
37 sisted, the more widely they published it. ·Their
      admiration was unbounded. "He has done all
      things well," they said, "he makes the deaf hear
      and the dumb speak."

✠

As we noted in the Introduction, the geographical
route described in verse 31 is at best confused (the
English has "improved" Mark's Greek here), and
probably is intended simply to return Jesus from the
"territory of Tyre" (verse 24).

Mark's Greek gives a different flavor from the English at some other points. In verse 33 the Greek simply
says, "Jesus spat and touched his tongue." Saliva is not
mentioned. In verse 35, "ligament" would better be
translated "bondage," a word associated with demonic
impediments. Thus Jesus freed the tongue from unnatu-

ral bondage, rather than from a restricting "ligament." The presence of a word in a foreign language (*ephphatha*) and mention of Jesus' sighing (verse 34) similarly belong to the common parlance of healings by demonic expulsion. The story may thus originally have been intended as a further example of Jesus' power over Satan.

There is a distinct flavor of the Old Testament about the story as well. The word describing the speech impediment in verse 32 is found only one other place in the Greek Bible, Isaiah 35:6, a passage (Is 35:5–6) to which verse 37 may also point. In Isaiah these verses point to the final times and God's salvation. Jesus is thus pictured as an agent of God's final deliverance.

Mark may also be responsible for verse 36, which shows that despite Jesus' apparent desire not to be known as a miracle-worker, his fame nevertheless spread widely (cf. 5:42, where the same idea is implied).

STUDY QUESTION: How important for our understanding of Jesus' act in this story is it to understand him in terms of Isaiah 35:5–6?

8:1–10
Jesus feeds many with little—again!

¹ 8 And now once again a great crowd had gathered, and they had nothing to eat. So he called
² his disciples to him and said to them, •"I feel sorry for all these people; they have been with me

3 for three days now and have nothing to eat. ·If I
send them off home hungry they will collapse on
4 the way; some have come a great distance." ·His
disciples replied, "Where could anyone get bread
to feed these people in a deserted place like this?"
5 He asked them, "How many loaves have you?"
6 "Seven," they said. ·Then he instructed the crowd
to sit down on the ground, and he took the seven
loaves, and after giving thanks he broke them and
handed them to his disciples to distribute; and
7 they distributed them among the crowd. ·They
had a few small fish as well, and over these he said
a blessing and ordered them to be distributed also.
8 They ate as much as they wanted, and they collected seven basketfuls of the scraps left over.
9 Now there had been about four thousand people.
10 He sent them away ·and immediately, getting into
the boat with his disciples, went to the region of
Dalmanutha.

✠

The remarks by Jesus (verses 2–3) and the reply by
the disciples (verse 4), unimaginable if the events recorded in 6:35–44 had in fact already occurred, make
it clear that this is another account of the same event
recorded there. While there are similarities, striking at
times, between the two stories, there are also a number
of differences in detail. Here the problem is a deserted
location (verse 4); in chapter 6 the problem was lack
of money (6:37). Here people have been with Jesus a
long time (verse 2); there it was late in the day
(6:35). Here Jesus began the discussion (verse 2);
there the disciples did (6:35). Here there were seven
loaves and a "few" fish (verses 5, 7), there five loaves
and two fish (6:38). Here seven baskets of fragments

are collected (verse 8), there twelve (6:43); and the words for "basket" differ. Here four thousand are fed (verse 9), there five thousand (6:44). Yet despite such differences, the overall impression left by the two stories is so similar one must wonder why Mark would choose to include both in his Gospel, even if both were present in his sources.

The absence of any indication of place in verse 1 makes it unlikely that Mark intended this feeding to be understood as occurring on gentile soil, thus showing Jesus feeding the gentiles, with the feeding of the five thousand then understood as occurring on Jewish soil, showing Jesus feeding the Jews, in that way having Jesus bring the "bread of life" (a non-Markan term) to all men. Rather, as 8:17–21 will show, Mark uses both feedings as prime examples of the stunning inability of the disciples to grasp the significance of Jesus on the basis of the wondrous acts they have seen him perform. As later parts of the Gospel will make clear, only knowledge of Jesus' suffering, and the resolve to endure if necessary the same fate in one's own life, enable one fully to understand the meaning of Jesus. Mark found in these two stories an occasion to emphasize that point.

It is worth noting that if we had only one of these stories, we would be tempted to account for the vivid detail by attributing it to an eye-witness description. The equally vivid yet different details in the two stories, coupled with the psychological improbability of verses 2–4 if this latter account were the second such historical occurrence, show that such details belong not to historical reminiscence but rather to the storyteller's art. That probably applies also to verse 10: There is no other record anywhere of a "Dalmanutha."

STUDY QUESTION: Compare both feedings with John
6:1–15. What can you say on the
basis of such a comparison about
the different point each story may
intend to make?

8:11–21
Jesus in the midst of misunderstanding

11   The Pharisees came up and started a discussion
      with him; they demanded of him a sign from
12   heaven, to test him. ·And with a sigh that came
      straight from the heart he said, "Why does this
      generation demand a sign? I tell you solemnly, no
13   sign shall be given to this generation." ·And leav-
      ing them again and re-embarking he went away
      to the opposite shore.
14   The disciples had forgotten to take any food
      and they had only one loaf with them in the boat.
15   Then he gave them this warning, "Keep your eyes
      open; be on your guard against the yeast of the
16   Pharisees and the yeast of Herod." ·And they said
      to one another, "It is because we have no bread."
17   And Jesus knew it, and he said to them, "Why are
      you talking about having no bread? Do you not yet
      understand? Have you no perception? Are your
18   minds closed? ·Have you eyes that do not see, ears
19   that do not hear? Or do you not remember? ·When
      I broke the five loaves among the five thousand,
      how many baskets full of scraps did you collect?"
20   They answered, "Twelve." ·"And when I broke
      the seven loaves for the four thousand, how many
      baskets full of scraps did you collect?" And they
21   answered, "Seven." ·Then he said to them, "Are
      you still without perception?"

✠

This episode, for which the signs of Markan editorial activity are abundant, is one of the more difficult in the whole Gospel. The context is not always smooth (the logical connection of verses 14 to 16 is obscure) and the meaning is difficult. (What does "sign from heaven" mean? To what does "leaven" refer? What is it the disciples should have understood from the two feedings?) The changes Matthew and Luke made in this passage show that even they found it hard to understand in its present form (cf. Mt 16:1–12; Lk 12:1, 54–56).

The Pharisees' request for a "sign from heaven" probably meant Jesus was required to say beforehand what he would do, or was asked to predict some future event, so that the divine origin of the results could then be verified (cf. Dt 18:21–22). This is clearly counter to all Jesus intends to do. He does all he can to avoid being understood as wonder-worker or soothsayer, as his response makes clear. Jesus will not give the impression God stands ready to do his bidding.

The saying in verse 15 is probably to be understood in relation to the Pharisees' question. Such a temptation to Jesus to act the part of a wonder-worker is perhaps the "leaven" (in Jewish references "leaven" virtually always has an evil connotation) his followers are to avoid. (For other interpretations, cf. Lk 11:29–30; Mt 12:39–40.) This warning Mark has included in the discussion about lack of bread. How the disciples could worry about a shortage of bread in light of the two wondrous feedings is all but incomprehensible. That appears to be Mark's point, however, and it becomes abundantly clear through the questions Jesus asks in verses 19–20. In light of all the bread provided, eaten,

and left over, how can they still be preoccupied with
arguments about lack of food? By thus failing to understand who the Jesus whom they accompany is, they
have put themselves into the ranks of those "outside,"
to whom all things appear confused and misleading
(the language of verse 18 is clearly reminiscent of
4:11–12). This episode confirms 6:52. Not even Jesus'
closest companions have understood who he really is.

These verses end the third segment of Mark's Gospel. As in the case of the first (1:1 to 3:6) and second
(3:7 to 6:6) segments, this one too ends on a negative
note. Just as the Pharisees (3:1–6) and Jesus' own
people (6:1–6) failed to understand, so the disciples
now include themselves in the same group. The career
of Jesus is clearly headed for tragedy. Only divine in-
tervention, it would seem, can rescue his life from failure. That is exactly the point toward which Mark is
moving his narrative.

STUDY QUESTIONS: If there were some symbolic meaning to "bread" in this segment,
what do you think it would be?
Can you find in Mark's narrative
thus far anything that would justify
finding here a symbolic meaning?
Anything to argue against such a
meaning?

Jesus Opens Blind Eyes:
Teachings on the Life of Discipleship
Mark 8:22 to 10:52

Mark 8:22–26
OPENING EVENT:
JESUS HEALS BLIND EYES

22 They came to Bethsaida, and some people
brought to him a blind man whom they begged
23 him to touch. ·He took the blind man by the hand
and led him outside the village. Then putting spittle on his eyes and laying his hands on him, he
24 asked, "Can you see anything?" ·The man, who
was beginning to see, replied, "I can see people;
they look like trees to me, but they are walking
25 about." ·Then he laid his hands on the man's eyes
again and he saw clearly; he was cured, and he
26 could see everything plainly and distinctly. ·And
Jesus sent him home, saying, "Do not even go into
the village."

✠

With this story, Mark begins the fourth segment of
his Gospel, a segment which is also concluded with an
account of curing blindness (10:46–52). The content
of this segment centers on instructions to Jesus' disciples and is organized around the three passion predictions (8:31; 9:31; 10:33–34). This story therefore begins a segment in which the disciples, who have just
shown themselves blind to the events in which they
have participated (see especially 8:11–21), have it

made clear to them who Jesus is and what their response as disciples must be.

The significance of this story must be derived from its placement in Mark's narrative rather than from any hints in the content. There is no mention of faith, nor any wondering assessment of Jesus. It could be told of any wonder-worker of the Greco-Roman world with only the change of the name. The twofold attempt to effect the cure simply emphasizes the difficulty faced by Jesus in this healing and is not unusual in Hellenistic miracle stories.

In its present context, however, it may well point to the difficulty Jesus experienced in curing the "blindness" of his disciples about who he was and what they had to become as his followers. It is perhaps too fanciful to equate their life with him during his earthly career as the first attempt to "cure" their "blindness," the resurrection as the second and successful attempt. Yet surely Mark felt it appropriate to place this story at this point in his narrative because it did show how hard it was for Jesus, at this juncture, to cure this stubborn case of blindness.

STUDY QUESTION: Neither Matthew nor Luke used this story in their Gospels. Why do you suppose they omitted it?

Mark 8:27 to 9:29
FIRST PASSION PREDICTION AND ATTENDANT EVENTS

8:27–33
Who understands Jesus correctly?

27 Jesus and his disciples left for the villages around Caesarea Philippi. On the way he put this question to his disciples, "Who do people say I
28 am?" ·And they told him. "John the Baptist," they said, "others Elijah; others again, one of the
29 prophets." ·"But you," he asked, "who do you say I am?" Peter spoke up and said to him, "You are
30 the Christ." ·And he gave them strict orders not to tell anyone about him.
31 And he began to teach them that the Son of Man was destined to suffer grievously, to be rejected by the elders and the chief priests and the scribes, and to be put to death, and after three days
32 to rise again; ·and he said all this quite openly. Then, taking him aside, Peter started to remon-
33 strate with him. ·But, turning and seeing his disciples, he rebuked Peter and said to him, "Get behind me, Satan! Because the way you think is not God's way but man's."

✠

This passage is the first in Mark's Gospel that deals directly and openly with Jesus' final fate, but it also shows how blind the disciples still are (cf. 8:22–26). Though Peter, here as so often spokesman-representative for the Twelve, is able to answer Jesus' question about his identity with an affirmation more appropriate than that accorded to Jesus by other "people" (verses 27–28; cf. 6:14–15), his reaction to the announcement that Jesus must suffer betrays the position he occupies: satanic opposition to God's will (verse 33).

Verse 30 by its content, and verses 31–32 by their language, show Markan editorial activity. If verse 33 originally followed verse 29, it showed a more negative reaction to the title "Christ" than is evident in the present context. Yet verse 30, with its typical Markan injunction to silence, makes clear that that title can only be misleading until after Easter, when cross and resurrection have made it evident that national, even military, aspirations, so often associated with that title, are no longer appropriate when applied to Jesus. Only when "Christ" (literally "anointed one," long expected by the Jews as glorious king) is interpreted as the "Son of Man" who must suffer, can it be appropriate.

The prediction of Jesus' suffering and resurrection (verse 31) probably has been influenced in its language by memories of Jesus' actual fate and by theological reflections by early Christians. While Jesus may well have intimated to his disciples that his fate included violent death at the hands of Jewish religious and legal authorities, the confusion of the disciples on Good Friday, and their disbelief at the news on Easter morning, would be all but incomprehensible if Jesus had foretold his fate as clearly as this.

The title "Son of Man," used only by Jesus of himself in Mark's Gospel, is of uncertain origin and meaning. Some earlier uses indicate humility (e.g., Ps 8:4;

Ezk 2:1), some grandeur (e.g., Dn 7:13–14). Whatever its original content may have been, in Jesus' mouth in the Gospels it is regularly associated with Jesus' death and resurrection and his future coming as judge. Scholars have reached no agreement on whether, or in what sense, the title was used by Jesus himself. But on one point there is clarity. In Mark it is a key to the true meaning of Jesus. For that reason, this passage is the first in a longer segment of Mark's Gospel which is designed to make clear to the reader who Jesus is and how we are to respond to him.

STUDY QUESTIONS: Verse 33 employs language often used in stories of expulsion of demons. Do you think Mark understood Peter's rebuke of Jesus (verse 32) to be demonic in origin? Are there other instances where disciples' misunderstandings could have been thought demonic?

8:34 to 9:1
Discipleship means losing to win

34 He called the people and his disciples to him and said, "If anyone wants to be a follower of mine, let him renounce himself and take up his 35 cross and follow me. ·For anyone who wants to save his life will lose it; but anyone who loses his life for my sake, and for the sake of the gospel, 36 will save it. ·What gain, then, is it for a man to win 37 the whole world and ruin his life? ·And indeed

what can a man offer in exchange for his life?
38 For if anyone in this adulterous and sinful generation is ashamed of me and of my words, the Son of
Man will also be ashamed of him when he comes
in the glory of his Father with the holy angels."

1 9 And he said to them, "I tell you solemnly,
there are some standing here who will not taste
death before they see the kingdom of God come
with power."

✠

If "nothing succeeds like success," what is left over
for failure? Peter, representing all humanity, made the
answer plain: avoid it (8:32)! Follow a man headed
for disgrace on a cross? Unimaginable! Yet these verses
make equally plain that anyone who would follow Jesus
must also be prepared to share his fate. What that
means these verses set out to explore.

In the first instance, it means living a life of giving,
not getting (verse 34; cf. 10:45). The opposite of such
a life is preoccupation with ourselves (verse 35), and
such preoccupation, in whatever form, religious or psychological, means closing ourselves off from the needs
of others. That, says Jesus, is to lose the point of life
(verse 36). Even gaining the world at the price of losing one's life is a poor bargain (verse 37). Yet our
whole culture so urges us on to become the "man who
has everything" that these words represent a total reversal of our values (cf. Ph 3:7–8). Such a deliberate
reversal is what "repentance" means. It means turning
away from one set of values and accepting another.
These verses thus make concrete what Mark began
with as a summary of Jesus' message: "Repent, and believe in the good news" (1:15). This reversal of values

which occurs when we follow Christ is not a matter of indifference. One's eternal fate hangs in the balance (verse 38). When God in Christ hangs on a cross, it brings the whole world to that decision: for him or against him.

Mark, who has assembled these verses, adds 9:1 to emphasize the urgency. In foreshortened prophetic expectation, Jesus announced the visible rule of God (the "kingdom of God come with power") within the lifetime of his generation. Like the prophets before him, Jesus saw the future but misinterpreted the speed at which it was coming. If that means he did not know when the kingdom was coming, it is no more than he himself admitted (13:32). Whatever the timetable, however, Christ crucified and risen is the key to God's future, and following him is the only way to have a share in it.

STUDY QUESTION: In what concrete ways is it possible for us to renounce ourselves and follow our crucified Lord?

9:2–8
A glimpse into the future

2   Six days later, Jesus took with him Peter and James and John and led them up a high mountain where they could be alone by themselves. There in
3   their presence he was transfigured: ·his clothes became dazzlingly white, whiter than any earthly
4   bleacher could make them. ·Elijah appeared to them with Moses; and they were talking with

5 Jesus. ·Then Peter spoke to Jesus: "Rabbi," he
said, "it is wonderful for us to be here; so let us
make three tents, one for you, one for Moses and
6 one for Elijah." ·He did not know what to say;
7 they were so frightened. ·And a cloud came, cov-
ering them in shadow; and there came a voice
from the cloud, "This is my Son, the Beloved.
8 Listen to him." ·Then suddenly, when they looked
around, they saw no one with them any more but
only Jesus.

☩

By his placement of this story, Mark portrays divine
confirmation of Jesus' statement about his future
(8:31). His suffering is in accord with God's will, and
its result will be heavenly glory for Jesus.

Speculation about where the "high mountain" was
located is pointless. A mountain is the traditional place
where divine revelations take place (cf. Ex 24:12; 1 K
19:11). The reference to "six days" is also unclear.
The point of the story is to be found in verse 3, where,
in details borrowed from expectations associated with
the last times, Jesus' final glory is seen, and in verse 7,
where God himself confirms that this Jesus must be listened to when he speaks of his own fate (8:31) and
that of his followers (8:34–38). Elijah and Moses may
be intended to show that law (Moses) and prophets
(Elijah) bear witness to Jesus, but they too are more
likely intended to point to final times (cf. Dt 18:15;
Ml 3:22–23 [= 4:4–5]).

Peter, again spokesman (this time for the "inner
three"; cf. 5:37; 13:3; 14:33), suggests action probably intended to prolong this experience of heavenly
glory. That it is as inappropriate as his previous reac-

tion (8:32) is shown by the negative interpretation of
the suggestion (verse 6).

The cloud, typically associated in the Bible with
God's presence, is also a divine vehicle in the final
events (cf. 13:26; 14:62), and continues the imagery
of ultimate glory. The abrupt ending following God's
declaration (addressed this time not to Jesus, as in
1:11, but to the disciples) shows this to be the climax.
Until the end, Jesus' words (verse 7: "Listen to him")
are all we have of such glory.

STUDY QUESTION: Do you think Mark intended this
                story as a glimpse of Jesus' coming
                resurrection, or of his final coming
                at the end of time?

9:9–13
Elijah and the coming cross

9 As they came down from the mountain he
   warned them to tell no one what they had seen,
   until after the Son of Man had risen from the
10 dead. ·They observed the warning faithfully,
   though among themselves they discussed what
11 "rising from the dead" could mean. ·And they put
   this question to him, "Why do the scribes say that
12 Elijah has to come first?" ·"True," he said, "Elijah
   is to come first and to see that everything is as it
   should be; yet how is it that the scriptures say
   about the Son of Man that he is to suffer griev-
13 ously and be treated with contempt? ·However,
   I tell you that Elijah has come and they have

treated him as they pleased, just as the scriptures say about him."

✠

There are points in this passage in Mark where the logical sequence, as indeed the wording itself, is not entirely clear. For example, a clearer sequence would be obtained if we simply omitted verses 2–10 and read verse 11 immediately after verse 1. Some have even suggested that that was the way Mark's source read, and that Mark disturbed the sequence when he inserted here the story of Jesus transfigured. Again, verses 9–10 clearly bear a Markan message: Only after the resurrection can the true nature of Jesus, and his full glory, be understood. Until that time, events such as the transfiguration are not to be discussed publicly. That the disciples persist in their inability to understand Jesus prior to that time is emphasized in verse 10.

If the connection between verses 9–10 and 11–13 is not entirely clear, the point of those latter verses is. If, as Malachi 4:4–5 says, Elijah comes before the final times, how could Jesus be Messiah if Elijah has not yet come? The answer: Elijah has already appeared in John the Baptist. But John/Elijah suffered and died at the hands of violent men, as Scripture had said. If, then, Scripture also says the Son of Man will suffer, how can that be doubted? Mark has shaped here yet another prediction of the suffering of Jesus.

One point does emerge from these verses, however. Jesus' glory, just seen, cannot be understood until after the Son of Man has fulfilled the suffering written of him and risen from the dead. That is a point Mark never tires of making.

STUDY QUESTION: Why do you think Mark felt it so important to connect Jesus' glory with his suffering?

9:14–29
Jesus cures a boy possessed

14 When they rejoined the disciples they saw a large crowd around them and some scribes argu-
15 ing with them. ·The moment they saw him the whole crowd were struck with amazement and ran
16 to greet him. ·"What are you arguing about with
17 them?" he asked. ·A man answered him from the crowd, "Master, I have brought my son to you;
18 there is a spirit of dumbness in him, ·and when it takes hold of him it throws him to the ground, and he foams at the mouth and grinds his teeth and goes rigid. And I asked your disciples to cast it out
19 and they were unable to." ·"You faithless genera-tion," he said to them in reply. "How much longer must I be with you? How much longer must I put
20 up with you? Bring him to me." ·They brought the boy to him, and as soon as the spirit saw Jesus it threw the boy into convulsions, and he fell to the ground and lay writhing there, foaming at the
21 mouth. ·Jesus asked the father, "How long has this been happening to him?" "From childhood,"
22 he replied, ·"and it has often thrown him into the fire and into the water, in order to destroy him. But if you can do anything, have pity on us and
23 help us." ·"If you can?" retorted Jesus. "Every-
24 thing is possible for anyone who has faith." ·Im-mediately the father of the boy cried out, "I do
25 have faith. Help the little faith I have!" ·And when

Jesus saw how many people were pressing around him, he rebuked the unclean spirit. "Deaf and dumb spirit," he said, "I command you: come out
26 of him and never enter him again." ·Then throwing the boy into violent convulsions it came out shouting, and the boy lay there so like a corpse
27 that most of them said, "He is dead." ·But Jesus took him by the hand and helped him up, and he
28 was able to stand. ·When he had gone indoors his disciples asked him privately, "Why were we un-
29 able to cast it out?" ·"This is the kind," he answered, "that can only be driven out by prayer."

☩

Some of the details in this complex story are common to accounts of exorcisms that circulated in the Greco-Roman world: the demonic aberrations in behavior, sometimes self-destructive; the command to the demon to leave and not return; the evidence of the violent exit of the demon. Some other details, however, which are confusing and even contradictory, cannot be explained that way. There are, for example, two descriptions of the illness (verses 17–18 and verse 22); the crowd is present (verse 14) but later assembles (verse 25—the translation has obscured the problem present in the Greek); the symptoms of the illness given in verses 18, 20, and 22 have nothing to do with deafness (verse 25) or dumbness (verses 17, 25); and the disciples who figure so prominently in verses 14–19 disappear completely in verses 20–27. Such confusions have led scholars to think this may be an early combination of two similar miracle stories, one of which contrasted the disciples' impotence with Jesus' power, and the other which contrasted the father's imperfect faith with Jesus' healing response.

There are some other unclear details—the reason for
the amazement of the crowd (verse 15) is not given,
and it is not clear to whom the words about the
"faithless generation" (verse 19) refer (disciples? bystanders? the father?). But in its present shape, the
story deals with faith, and primarily with Jesus' ability
to perform his healing deeds despite its absence. Not
only the disciples but even the father lacks the kind of
faith Jesus seeks (the translation of verse 24 distorts
the Greek; "help my unfaith" or "lack of faith" is
closer to its intention). Nowhere is there any hint that
the father finally did achieve sufficient faith. The point
is rather that God's power at work in Jesus is so strong
that neither imperfect (verse 24) nor even absent
(verse 19) faith can thwart it.

Perhaps that is the reason Mark gave this combined
story an introduction (verse 14) and a conclusion
(verses 28–29) and put it in this section of his Gospel
dealing with instructions to the disciples. That final reference to prayer tells us that the only appropriate response to Jesus is total, trusting reliance on God's
power, which is the attitude of prayer as well as of faith.
Yet the story also assures us that however imperfect
our faith may be, Jesus is nevertheless able to overcome the evil forces at work within our lives.

STUDY QUESTION: Why do you suppose Mark thought
                this was an appropriate story to
                place after the account of the
                transfiguration?

Mark 9:30 to 10:31
SECOND PASSION PREDICTION
AND ATTENDANT EVENTS

9:30–32
A second formal passion prediction

30 After leaving that place they made their way through Galilee; and he did not want anyone to
31 know, ·because he was instructing his disciples; he was telling them, "The Son of Man will be delivered into the hands of men; they will put him to death; and three days after he has been put to
32 death he will rise again." ·But they did not understand what he said and were afraid to ask him.

✠

Mark continues here the pattern that he set with the first prediction of the passion and that he will continue with the third. After the prediction (8:31; 9:31; 10:33–34) there is a problem of misunderstanding (8:32–33; 9:33–34; 10:35–41) followed by instruction on the nature of discipleship (8:34–38; 9:35–37; 10:42–45). Interspersed are stories that reveal Jesus' true nature (9:2–8) and power (9:14–29, 38–41), and further teachings.

The details in this prediction show that even the most careful concentration on teaching the disciples (verses 30–31a) fails to achieve that goal (verse 32).

How difficult it was for the disciples to understand what it meant to follow Jesus! How difficult it remains for us to understand that!

STUDY QUESTION: The enemies of the Son of Man are men (i.e., human beings; verse 31). What does that irony say about the way people relate to God?

9:33–37
True greatness is humility

33   They came to Capernaum, and when he was in the house he asked them, "What were you arguing
34 about on the road?" ·They said nothing because they had been arguing which of them was the
35 greatest. ·So he sat down, called the Twelve to him and said, "If anyone wants to be first, he must
36 make himself last of all and servant of all." ·He then took a little child, set him in front of them,
37 put his arms around him, and said to them, ·"Anyone who welcomes one of these little children in my name, welcomes me; and anyone who welcomes me welcomes not me but the one who sent me."

✠

Unlike contemporary American culture, the Greco-Roman world saw no particular virtue in being a child. Powerless and helpless, a child was entirely at the mercy of the head of its family. It is in that context that these verses must be understood. As a correction to the disciples' dispute about which of them was greatest, a dispute that betrayed their total incomprehension of all Jesus had thus far said about his fate and about the proper acts and attitudes of those who would follow him, Jesus uses a child to illustrate the necessity of being concerned for the powerless, not the great. In an act that figures forth his point, he embraces a child, as he will later figure forth that point by embracing a cross.

Although this combination by Mark of originally independent sayings of Jesus is not without its difficulties (Jesus summons in verse 35 those who are already with him in the house, verse 33), the common point clearly has to do with the proper stance of a follower of Jesus. That proper stance is humility, not pride, a hard lesson for disciples to learn.

STUDY QUESTION: "Child" and "little one" are sometimes used for followers of Jesus (e.g., 9:42). In that light, what would verse 37 say about the attitudes Christians should have toward one another?

9:38–41
Who belongs to the "in-group"?

38 John said to him, "Master, we saw a man who is not one of us casting out devils in your name; and because he was not one of us we tried to stop

³⁹ him." ·But Jesus said, "You must not stop him:
no one who works a miracle in my name is likely
⁴⁰ to speak evil of me. ·Anyone who is not against
us is for us.

⁴¹   "If anyone gives you a cup of water to drink
just because you belong to Christ, then I tell you
solemnly, he will most certainly not lose his
reward."

☩

Mark continues to assemble the sayings of Jesus he
found in his tradition (Matthew and Luke also used
them but put them into other contexts they thought
more appropriate). Verses 38–40 point to a phenome-
non known in the time of the early church (see Ac
19:13–14) and perhaps equally likely to have occurred
during Jesus' lifetime. The astonishing thing here is the
open and tolerant attitude displayed. Like the warning
against personal arrogance (verses 33–37), these
verses speak against any kind of group arrogance. Even
a minor helpful gesture toward one who follows Jesus
will be favorably noted by God (verse 41). Thus no
one who takes Jesus seriously is to be despised, as
nothing positive done in his name is to be forbidden by
those who follow him.

STUDY QUESTION: Do these verses have any application to contemporary definitions of
"Christian" and "church"?

9:42–50
Above all else, God's will

42   "But anyone who is an obstacle to bring down
      one of these little ones who have faith, would be
      better thrown into the sea with a great millstone
43   around his neck. ·And if your hand should cause
      you to sin, cut it off; it is better for you to enter
      into life crippled, than to have two hands and go
45   to hell, into the fire that cannot be put out. ·And
      if your foot should cause you to sin, cut it off; it
      is better for you to enter into life lame, than to
47   have two feet and be thrown into hell. ·And if
      your eye should cause you to sin, tear it out; it
      is better for you to enter into the kingdom of God
      with one eye, than to have two eyes and be thrown
48   into hell ·where their worm does not die nor
49   their fire go out. ·For everyone will be salted with
50   fire. ·Salt is a good thing, but if salt has become
      insipid, how can you season it again? Have salt in
      yourselves and be at peace with one another."

✠

Whether Mark or his tradition combined these
verses, the reasons for their combination are not always
clear. Verses 42–48 center around the expression
"cause to sin" ("an obstacle to bring down" in verse 42
translates the same Greek word that is translated "cause
to sin" in verses 43, 45, and 47). Verse 49 seems connected by the word "fire" to verse 48, and verse 50 by
the word "salt" to verse 49. Such word associations
were probably an aid in memorizing such groups of say-

ings. From verse 42 we also learn that the "little ones" who are so utterly dependent (see comments on verses 33–37) are those who depend as much on God in faith as little children depend on their fathers.

The figure of a millstone around the neck is a poetic exaggeration to make a point. Such exaggeration is then continued in the following verses (for other examples, see 10:25; Mt 7:4–5, 9; 23:24). The point is not advice on self-mutilation, as though such extraordinary deeds would earn extraordinary rewards. Rather, it is a radical way of making the point that obeying God, and thus remaining in fellowship with him, is so important that nothing, even what we might otherwise regard as indispensable, is to stand in its way.

The word for "hell" is derived from the Hebrew word for "Valley of Hinnom," a place south of Jerusalem where human sacrifices had once been offered to the god Molech (2 K 23:10; Jr 32:35). Desecrated by King Josiah, it became the city dump for Jerusalem, and a figure for the place of final judgment (see Jr 7:32; 19:6). Verse 48, drawn from Isaiah 66:24, also reflects such an image, which again points to the seriousness which attaches to obeying and disobeying God.

The references to salt in verses 49–50 are unclear, precisely because salt had so many symbolic meanings —among them sacrifice, preservation, purification, and fellowship. Verse 49 could refer to trials Christians would have to undergo, even to the point of self-sacrifice (cf. Lk 14:26–27; Mk 8:34). Another form of verse 50a is found in Matthew 5:13. Perhaps the point of both is a warning against laxity in discipleship. If salt means fellowship in verse 50b, it could be advice on maintaining a peaceful community. But we simply cannot be sure anymore what meaning was intended.

STUDY QUESTION: Can you think of figurative images other than those used in verses 43–47 by means of which to describe in more contemporary terms the importance of obeying God?

10:1–12
The seriousness of marriage

¹ **10** Leaving there, he came to the district of Judaea and the far side of the Jordan. And again crowds gathered around him, and again he ² taught them, as his custom was. ·Some Pharisees approached him and asked, "Is it against the law for a man to divorce his wife?" They were testing ³ him. ·He answered them, "What did Moses com- ⁴ mand you?" ·"Moses allowed us," they said, "to draw up a writ of dismissal and so to divorce." ⁵ Then Jesus said to them, "It was because you were so unteachable that he wrote this commandment ⁶ for you. ·But from the beginning of creation God ⁷ made them male and female. ·This is why a man ⁸ must leave father and mother, ·and the two be- come one body. They are no longer two, there- ⁹ fore, but one body. ·So then, what God has united, ¹⁰ man must not divide." ·Back in the house the dis- ¹¹ ciples questioned him again about this, ·and he said to them, "The man who divorces his wife and marries another is guilty of adultery against her. ¹² And if a woman divorces her husband and mar- ries another she is guilty of adultery too."

✠

This section of Mark's Gospel appears to be a collection of instructions to Jesus' followers on how they are to live in regard to marriage (verses 1–12), children (verses 13–16), and wealth (verses 17–27). They also show that Jesus is not being forced to travel to Jerusalem. He moves willingly to the fate that awaits him there (cf. 8:31; 9:31).

There was considerable dispute among lawyers in the Judaism of Jesus' time about valid reasons for divorce. Should it be entered into only for the most serious causes (e.g., unchastity, adultery), or could it be accomplished for any reason at all (e.g., too much salt in the food the wife prepared)? That divorce was permitted to the husband (though not to the wife) was assumed on the basis of Deuteronomy 24:1–4. Whether they wanted to test Jesus' knowledge of the law or wanted to test whether he would set himself against the law of Moses (verse 2) is not clear.

Jesus answered by setting one part of the Jewish Scripture (Gn 1:27; 2:24) above another (Dt 24:1). The import of Jesus' words is clear. The sexual union sanctified in the marriage bond is grounded in creation, and hence is not sinful, but rather reflects God's merciful will for his creatures. That bond, once entered into, is not lightly to be ruptured.

To the Pharisees' question, therefore, of what is *allowed* (verse 4, and implied in verse 2), Jesus responds in terms of what God has *commanded* (verse 3, implied in verse 7). To a question designed to find the outer limits of activity that could still be considered lawful, Jesus answered in terms of the true intention of God.

To this dispute, Mark has appended in verses 10–12 another saying which makes the same point. The form of verse 12 is possible only under Roman law, where, unlike Jewish legal custom, a woman could also initiate divorce. St. Paul quotes a similarly adapted form of this saying of Jesus (1 Co 7:10–11). Clearly, then, when the early Christian community faced a new legal situation as it carried its mission to the gentiles, it felt this saying about marriage was so important it had to be adapted so that its original intention would not be lost. Thus, verses 11–12 simply reinforce the point of verses 2–9. Marriage is willed by God, and neither husband nor wife may be exempted from the seriousness of maintaining the marriage bond intact.

In a society like ours which is disturbed to the point of psychosis by the problem of divorce, these words of Jesus help us see the root of the problem. Marriages entered into hastily and for frivolous reasons, which mock the serious, even sacred nature of the marriage union, are the cause of many of our problems. The question for us can never be "How much can we get away with?" It must always be "What is God's gracious and merciful will for his creation?" Only that question will allow us to formulate answers that do not go counter to God's mercy to us and to all creation.

STUDY QUESTION: Perhaps more sharply in this passage than in any other, the words of Jesus stand in judgment on the easy moral solutions embodied in our culture, in this case concerning divorce. Do you think more stringent laws will solve the problem?

10:13–16
As a child, or not at all

13 People were bringing little children to him, for him to touch them. The disciples turned them
14 away, ·but when Jesus saw this he was indignant and said to them, "Let the little children come to me; do not stop them; for it is to such as these
15 that the kingdom of God belongs. ·I tell you solemnly, anyone who does not welcome the kingdom of God like a little child will never enter it."
16 Then he put his arms around them, laid his hands on them and gave them his blessing.

✠

Contrary to a rabbinic saying, which saw attention to children, like drinking too much wine or associating with the ignorant, as a pernicious waste of time, Jesus rebuked his disciples for driving off (the translation softens their act) some children. Rather, says Jesus, they are models for the way into the kingdom. At issue is not a child's natural innocence or purity, let alone its intellectual docility or even ignorance. A child in Jesus' culture "deserved" nothing, had no claim on anyone for wages or reward. If a child was well treated, it was because of the love and generosity of the parent. So we receive the kingdom of God, Jesus says, as a gift of grace, not as something fully deserved or clearly earned, or we don't receive it, or enter it, at all. The blessing by Jesus that follows shows that acceptance by him is tantamount to such entry.

STUDY QUESTION: Who occupy the place in our culture that children did in the culture of Jesus? People on welfare? the handicapped? the aged? some other group?

10:17–22
A rich man in trouble

17 He was setting out on a journey when a man ran up, knelt before him and put this question to him, "Good master, what must I do to inherit 18 eternal life?" ·Jesus said to him, "Why do you call 19 me good? No one is good but God alone. ·You know the commandments: You must not kill; You must not commit adultery; You must not steal; You must not bring false witness; You must not defraud; Honor your father and mother." 20 And he said to him, "Master, I have kept all these 21 from my earliest days." ·Jesus looked steadily at him and loved him, and he said, "There is one thing you lack. Go and sell everything you own and give the money to the poor, and you will have 22 treasure in heaven; then come, follow me." ·But his face fell at these words and he went away sad, for he was a man of great wealth.

✠

By his question, the man (no hint in Mark he was young) shows his awareness that more is necessary before God than just following rules. Otherwise, since he had done that all his life, he would not have asked Jesus how to gain eternal life. Jesus' response is

difficult for those who know him as risen Savior. Surely
he is good! Yet Jesus during his earthly life never confused himself with the Father (verse 18b), and when
Jesus here, as he so often did, spoke and acted for God
(cf. 2:1–12; 4:35–41; 10:13–16), he nevertheless did
it in the consciousness that he was the Father's agent,
not the Father himself.

The command to sell all and give to the poor is not
intended to be one more rule, one which everyone must
follow. Jesus did not always require that everything be
sold to benefit the poor (cf. 14:3–9), nor that one had
to leave all to follow him (cf. 5:18–19). Rather, for
this man at *this* time, wealth was what hindered him
from becoming a follower of Jesus, and he was to be
rid of it, as anyone must be rid of anything which
hinders him or her from taking Jesus seriously. This
story does not intend to say that poverty is more
blessed than wealth, or that only the poor can be saved.
But it does say that nothing, including wealth, can be
allowed to stand in the way of our becoming followers
of Jesus.

STUDY QUESTION: What are some other hindrances besides wealth that can keep us from
becoming followers of Jesus?

10:23–27
Riches won't help with God

23   Jesus looked around and said to his disciples,
"How hard it is for those who have riches to
24   enter the kingdom of God!" ·The disciples were

astounded by these words, but Jesus insisted, "My
children," he said to them, "how hard it is to en-
25 ter the kingdom of God! ·It is easier for a camel
to pass through the eye of a needle than for a rich
26 man to enter the kingdom of God." ·They were
more astonished than ever. "In that case," they
27 said to one another, "who can be saved?" ·Jesus
gazed at them. "For men," he said, "it is impossible, but not for God: because everything is possible for God."

☩

If the kind of achievement that brings riches will not
qualify a person for entry into God's kingdom, neither
will any other kind of human achievement. That is the
point of verse 27, which climaxes this passage. Entry
into God's kingdom is by his grace, or it does not
occur. We may well share the disciples' astonishment at
that, but the two sayings of Jesus, the one in verse 24
without the qualification about riches, make it impossible to ignore. We have about as much chance of
achieving acceptance with God because of our accom-
plishments as a camel has of getting through a needle's
eye. The comparison is meant to picture impossibility.
The suggestion that Jesus originally said "hawser"
(*kamilos*) and someone later mistakenly substituted
"camel" (*kamelos*) helps little; a hawser won't go
through a needle's eye either. The fable about a narrow
gate in Jerusalem called "the Needle's Eye" which a
camel had great difficulty passing through is not
recorded until the ninth century. In their own way, such
attempts to get around this saying show its correct-
ness. How difficult it is to accept that only by God's
grace, not by our own virtues, do we have access to
him and his kingdom.

STUDY QUESTION: In Genesis 18:14 a phrase similar
to verse 27 describes a miracle. Is
our salvation to be understood similarly as a miracle?

10:28–31
True wealth and God's kingdom

28   Peter took this up. "What about us?" he asked
him. "We have left everything and followed you."
29   Jesus said, "I tell you solemnly, there is no one
who has left house, brothers, sisters, father, children or land for my sake and for the sake of the
30   gospel ·who will not be repaid a hundred times
over, houses, brothers, sisters, mothers, children
and land—not without persecutions—now in this
present time and in the world to come, eternal life.
31   "Many who are first will be last, and the last
first."

☩

If riches won't qualify one for the kingdom, following Jesus does not mean impoverishment. Verses
29–30 probably reflect, in their present wording, the
experience of Christian fellowship present in the primitive church: what one had, all had (cf. Ac 2:43–47;
4:32). What one therefore lost in order to follow Jesus
would be likewise gained by following him. The addition of the phrase about persecution (verse 30), and
the saying about the final reversal of values (verse 31)
nevertheless make clear that one must follow Jesus for
his sake, not for the sake of any material reward. The

absence of "wives" from verses 29–30 has caused much speculation. The omission is perhaps intentional. While the figure of many parents (father, verse 29; mothers, verse 30) is tolerable, the idea of many wives could only be misunderstood.

STUDY QUESTION: Is verse 31 appropriate as a concluding word for the whole section (9:30 to 10:30), or did Mark intend to restrict it to just these verses?

Mark 10:32–45
THIRD PASSION PREDICTION AND ATTENDANT EVENTS

10:32–34
Yet once more, the passion is predicted

32 They were on the road, going up to Jerusalem; Jesus was walking on ahead of them; they were in a daze, and those who followed were apprehensive. Once more taking the Twelve aside he began to tell them what was going to happen to him:
33 "Now we are going up to Jerusalem, and the Son of Man is about to be handed over to the chief priests and the scribes. They will condemn him to death and will hand him over to the pagans,
34 who will mock him and spit at him and scourge him and put him to death; and after three days he will rise again."

✠

With this third prediction of the passion, Mark begins once more his cycle of traditions: prediction, misunderstanding, and instructions about discipleship (the other two sections begin at 8:31 and 9:30). The detailed prediction (verses 33–34) appears influenced by knowledge of the actual events, and may have been shaped by liturgical or catechetical use. The word translated "dazed" in verse 32 was translated as "astonished" in 1:27 and "astounded" in 10:24. Either of those would be preferable here, since Mark's point appears to be the fear inspired by Jesus' resolute action in taking the way to Jerusalem, which must lead to his passion. Fear and astonishment regularly accompany the reception of divine revelation in biblical narratives, and Mark may want to give further notice that Jesus' fate accords with God's will.

STUDY QUESTION: Is there special significance that Jesus goes "ahead" of his disciples on the way to Jerusalem (cf. 14:28; 16:7)?

10:35–45
On "looking out for number one"

35   James and John, the sons of Zebedee, approached him. "Master," they said to him, "we
36   want you to do us a favor." ·He said to them,
37   "What is it you want me to do for you?" ·They said to him, "Allow us to sit one at your right hand and the other at your left in your glory."
38   "You do not know what you are asking," Jesus said to them. "Can you drink the cup that I must drink, or be baptized with the baptism with which
39   I must be baptized?" ·They replied, "We can." Jesus said to them, "The cup that I must drink you shall drink, and with the baptism with which
40   I must be baptized you shall be baptized, ·but as for seats at my right hand or my left, these are not mine to grant; they belong to those to whom they have been allotted."

⁴¹   When the other ten heard this they began to
⁴² feel indignant with James and John, ·so Jesus
called them to him and said to them, "You know
that among the pagans their so-called rulers lord
it over them, and their great men make their au-
⁴³ thority felt. ·This is not to happen among you. No;
anyone who wants to become great among you
⁴⁴ must be your servant, ·and anyone who wants to
⁴⁵ be first among you must be slave to all. ·For the
Son of Man himself did not come to be served
but to serve, and to give his life as a ransom for
many."

✠

Once again Mark has followed Jesus' prediction of
his coming death and resurrection with traditions that
show the inability of the disciples to understand what
that means, and some sayings of Jesus about true discipleship (cf. 8:31 to 9:1; 9:31–37). It was apparently
an important point for Mark.

The request from James and John for places of special honor receives several answers in the verses that
follow it. Honor comes only after suffering (verses
38–39). God, not Jesus, will determine such rankings
(the intention of verse 40). True honor means serving,
not ruling (verses 42–44). Entry into Jesus' "glory" is
by the same path for all: Christ's suffering on our be-
half (verse 45). It is thus apparent that our present
passage represents a collection of sayings on this theme,
rather than a verbatim historical record, although the
request of the sons of Zebedee may well rest on accurate memory.

It is also clear that Mark has shaped this passage in
light of its nearness to the account of Jesus' passion.
The reference to Jesus' glory is echoed in a saying of

Jesus during his trial (14:62), and the figure of a "cup" is used again by Jesus in his prayer in Gethsemane (14:36; that shows that verses 38–39 also refer to suffering). The final verse, a kind of capsule summary of Mark's understanding of Jesus, shared by other New Testament authors (cf. Rm 3:24–25; 1 Co 6:20; Ga 1:4; 3:13–14; Heb 2:17–18; 1 P 2:21, 24), is a fitting introduction to the story of Jesus' final days.

Perhaps the main intention of these verses is to say something about proper behavior within the church. We are to deal with one another (verses 42–44) as God has dealt with us in Christ (verse 45). That is what "following Christ" means. Rule in the church is therefore accomplished only by serving. That is especially significant in the light of the request made by James and John. High rank in the church is not a matter of glory and power; it is a matter of service, perhaps even of suffering, because that was the fate of the master of the church. In political life, rule goes to the powerful, and they use it for their own enrichment and comfort. "That is not to happen among you." Those who follow Christ must let that fact shape their total lives, in and out of church.

STUDY QUESTIONS: In the light of this passage, were the other ten disciples justified in being indignant with James and John? What is the proper way of dealing with people who insist on putting their own interests first?

Mark 10:46–52
CONCLUDING EVENT:
BLIND EYES HEALED

10:46–52
Faith cures blindness

⁴⁶ They reached Jericho; and as he left Jericho with his disciples and a large crowd, Bartimaeus (that is, the son of Timaeus), a blind beggar, was ⁴⁷ sitting at the side of the road. ·When he heard that it was Jesus of Nazareth, he began to shout and to say, "Son of David, Jesus, have pity on ⁴⁸ me." ·And many of them scolded him and told him to keep quiet, but he only shouted all the ⁴⁹ louder, "Son of David, have pity on me." ·Jesus stopped and said, "Call him here." So they called the blind man. "Courage," they said, "get up; he ⁵⁰ is calling you." ·So throwing off his cloak, he ⁵¹ jumped up and went to Jesus. ·Then Jesus spoke, "What do you want me to do for you?" "Rab-buni," the blind man said to him, "Master, let me ⁵² see again." ·Jesus said to him, "Go; your faith has saved you." And immediately his sight returned and he followed him along the road.

✠

The awkward language of the first verse, more apparent in the Greek than in our translation (the references to disciples and crowd are ungrammatically tacked on, and the entry and immediate departure from Jericho seem artificial), make it clear that Mark has adapted this story to its present context. The story is unique in Mark in several respects. It is the only miracle whose beneficiary is named, it is the only story where Jesus is called "Son of David" (in Jewish tradition, a descendant of David would be the Messiah), and it is the only story where the one healed follows Jesus. The final act of this kind to be reported in Mark, it serves as the climax of Jesus' ministry of healing and teaching, and as the transition to the account of Jesus' fate in Jerusalem.

It is with this story, then, that Mark concludes the fourth major segment of his Gospel. The segment ends, as it began (8:22–26), with a story of blindness healed. Since the segment contains the major portion of instruction to the disciples included in this Gospel, Mark probably intended the symbolism—namely, only those who experience the miracle of Jesus' power (most clearly expressed, for Mark, in cross and resurrection—hence the three predictions of the passion) have their eyes opened to his importance. The story adds another dimension to the reception of that "miracle." It is faith (verse 52). Such faith means to persist in calling upon Jesus despite any hindrance (verses 47–48), and then to follow him despite any threat ("along the road" in verse 52 is used by Mark to mean the way to Jerusalem and suffering).

STUDY QUESTION: What element in this story, do you think, made Mark deem it appropriate for use as the bridge between instruction of the disciples and Jesus' passion?

Jesus in Jerusalem
Mark 11:1 to 16:20

Mark 11:1 to 12:44
JESUS IN THE TEMPLE: ACTION AND REACTION

11:1–11
Jesus comes to Jerusalem

¹ 11 When they were approaching Jerusalem, in sight of Bethphage and Bethany, close by the Mount of Olives, he sent two of his disciples ² and said to them, "Go off to the village facing you, and as soon as you enter it you will find a tethered colt that no one has yet ridden. Untie it ³ and bring it here. ·If anyone says to you, 'What are you doing?' say, 'The Master needs it and will ⁴ send it back here directly.'" ·They went off and found a colt tethered near a door in the open ⁵ street. As they untied it, ·some men standing there said, "What are you doing, untying that ⁶ colt?" ·They gave the answer Jesus had told them, ⁷ and the men let them go. ·Then they took the colt to Jesus and threw their cloaks on its back, and ⁸ he sat on it. ·Many people spread their cloaks on the road, others greenery which they had cut in ⁹ the fields. ·And those who went in front and those who followed were all shouting, "Hosanna! Blessings on him who comes in the name of the Lord! ¹⁰ Blessings on the coming kingdom of our father ¹¹ David! Hosanna in the highest heavens!" ·He entered Jerusalem and went into the Temple. He looked all around him, but as it was now late, he went out to Bethany with the Twelve.

✠

We must be careful to read this story as Mark wrote
it, not as we know it from other Gospels. It is not a triumphal entry into Jerusalem (cf. verse 11), nor is there
any indication people from Jerusalem came out to take
part in the procession. The people involved are Jesus'
followers. They don't call Jesus "king," but refer instead to the coming of David's final kingdom (verse
10). Even the palm branches are missing. Rather, the
people scatter leaves and rushes from the fields in
Jesus' path (verse 8).

Though the two villages named do not have any particular significance (they lie about a mile and a half
apart on the road to Jerusalem), the reference to the
Mount of Olives does, since there was a tradition,
based on Zechariah 14:4, that the Messiah would appear there in the last times. That, coupled with the explicit references to the "colt," which recalled Zechariah
9:9, shows that Mark did see messianic significance in
this story. It is the appearance of the Messiah, but, typically for Mark, in such a form that even those who
saw it did not really understand it.

The directions Jesus gave his disciples, unless they
are intended to demonstrate Jesus' prophetic powers,
indicate Jesus was more familiar with this area than
Mark's narrative would have led us to believe. Either
way, the impression is clear that what happens is not
accidental. It happens as planned, a theme Mark has
continually emphasized with regard to Jesus' passion
(e.g., the repeated predictions of it).

The gesture of scattering garments and rushes in the
road announces Jesus as king (cf. 2 K 9:13), as does

his gesture of riding on a colt never before ridden; yet it is also clear that he comes not as a military hero mounted on a horse of war, but on a colt, as a messenger of God's peace (cf. Zc 9:9–10). The cry of the people is taken from Psalm 118:25–26, verses that belong to Scripture passages read by festival pilgrims during their morning prayers. But again, in Mark's perspective, "hosanna" (Hebrew: "Help us!" cf. Ps 118:25) addressed to Jesus has its ironic overtones. Jesus will do just that, but in a way that will cause those who now celebrate his coming to Jerusalem to fall away (see 14:50) in the very moment when the events that make such help possible (Jesus' death; cf. 10:45) begin to unfold. The story thus continues Mark's narrative of the career of Jesus who came as Messiah in such a way that, prior to his passion, he simply could not be fully understood.

STUDY QUESTION: Why would God's Messiah come in such a way as to remain hidden until his resurrection?

11:12–25
From the fig tree learn a lesson:
Jesus and the Temple

12   Next day as they were leaving Bethany, he felt
13   hungry. ·Seeing a fig tree in leaf some distance away, he went to see if he could find any fruit on it, but when he came up to it he found nothing
14   but leaves; for it was not the season for figs. ·And he addressed the fig tree. "May no one ever eat

fruit from you again," he said. And his disciples
heard him say this.

15   So they reached Jerusalem and he went into
the Temple and began driving out those who were
selling and buying there; he upset the tables of
the money changers and the chairs of those who
16   were selling pigeons. ·Nor would he allow anyone
17   to carry anything through the Temple. ·And he
taught them and said, "Does not scripture say:
My house will be called a house of prayer for all
the peoples? But you have turned it into a rob-
18   bers' den." ·This came to the ears of the chief
priests and the scribes, and they tried to find some
way of doing away with him; they were afraid of
him because the people were carried away by his
19   teaching. ·And when evening came he went out
of the city.

20   Next morning, as they passed by, they saw the
21   fig tree withered to the roots. ·Peter remembered.
"Look, Rabbi," he said to Jesus, "the fig tree
22   you cursed has withered away." ·Jesus answered,
23   "Have faith in God. ·I tell you solemnly, if anyone says to this mountain, 'Get up and throw
yourself into the sea,' with no hesitation in his
heart but believing that what he says will hap-
24   pen, it will be done for him. ·I tell you therefore:
everything you ask and pray for, believe that you
25   have it already, and it will be yours. ·And when
you stand in prayer, forgive whatever you have
against anybody, so that your Father in heaven
may forgive your failings too."

✠

By inserting one tradition (the Temple cleansing,
verses 15–19) into another (the fig tree cursed, verses
12–14, 20–25), it is clear Mark means us to see them
as interpreting one another (cf. 5:21–43 for a similar
combination of traditions). That means the fate of the

fig tree and of the Temple are the same. Jesus' "curse" means they will "die." That the fig tree did so the next day (verse 20) means the destruction of the Temple (cf. 13:2) is similarly certain.

The reason for the symbolic "destruction" of the Temple (verses 15–16) is given in verse 17. The reference to "a robbers' den" does not mean Jesus was irked at dishonest business practices by those who sold animals and changed money. He drove out the buyers as well (verse 15). More importantly, that phrase comes from Jeremiah 7:11, where it refers to the place where robbers retreat for safety *after* they have done their evil deeds. Jesus' accusation is directed not against sharp business practices but against the idea that no matter what people do, they are safe from punishment in the Temple (cf. Jr 7:9–15). Nor does Jesus have in mind merely a reform of Temple practices. Animals were necessary for cultic sacrifices, and only coins with no image (cf. Ex 20:4) could be used to pay Temple taxes. Both were present to aid Temple worshipers, but if no animals were available for sacrifice and if no money could be paid to support the Temple, the Temple could no longer function. With this act of prophetic protest, therefore, Jesus fulfilled the Old Testament predictions of the Temple's end because of the faithlessness of the chosen people (cf. Jr 7:12–15; Ho 9:15).

What the Temple was supposed to be was a house of worship "for all nations" (verse 17; cf. Is 56:7). It had not become that instrument of salvation, and so it had outlived its usefulness. Indeed, in God's plan, Jesus, not the Temple, is that "instrument." He is the one through whom salvation will be offered to gentiles, as his travels in their lands have already indicated (7:24, 31; 8:27). Thus, in God's plan, salvation through Jesus will be offered to all gentiles (or "nations"; the Greek word is the same) before God's kingdom comes (13:10; cf. Rm 11:25–26a). The Temple no longer figures in that plan.

That is probably the explanation of that strange phrase: "it was not the season for figs" (verse 13). The fig tree, symbolic of the Temple in their common curse and destruction (it is total; cf. "from its roots" in verse 20), here also symbolizes the place of the Temple in God's plan. There is no fruit on the fig tree because it is not the tree's proper time for that. Similarly, there is no fruit of salvation in the Temple—i.e., all nations worshiping there—because it is not the Temple's proper time for that, either. The "place" of salvation has been shifted from Temple to Jesus. Thus, in God's plan, the Temple is barren. This the barren fig tree also shows us symbolically. The "curse" (verse 14) is not due to Jesus' unreasonable expectations about figs. Mark means it to tell us more about the fate of the Temple.

That is probably also the reason for the final words about faith (verses 22–25). For Mark, faith is always tied to Jesus. Hence, faith-filled prayer is now related to Jesus, not the Temple. If we would find God in any effective way, it must be through Jesus, who now teaches us about prayer, not through a Temple whose time has passed. These verses show us how in God's plan God is to be found: in faithful prayer (verses 22–24) and in enacting God's loving forgiveness of us in our treatment of our fellow human beings (verse 25). In this combination of traditions, then, Mark tells us beforehand what he will make explicit in the remainder of his Gospel. Jesus, crucified and risen, is the only way to God.

STUDY QUESTIONS: Is there a "robbers' den" mentality apparent in some contemporary attitudes about participation in church activities? What would be a correct attitude toward such participation?

11:27–33
Temple authorities challenge Jesus

27 They came to Jerusalem again, and as Jesus was walking in the Temple, the chief priests and 28 the scribes and the elders came to him, ·and they said to him, "What authority have you for acting like this? Or who gave you authority to do these 29 things?" ·Jesus said to them, "I will ask you a question, only one; answer me and I will tell you 30 my authority for acting like this. ·John's baptism: did it come from heaven, or from man? 31 Answer me that." ·And they argued it out this way among themselves: "If we say from heaven, he will say, 'Then why did you refuse to believe 32 him?' ·But dare we say from man?"—they had the people to fear, for everyone held that John was a 33 real prophet. ·So their reply to Jesus was, "We do not know." And Jesus said to them, "Nor will I tell you my authority for acting like this."

✠

Some question about the authority that allowed Jesus to act as he had done in the Temple was inevitable, and the people who pose it to Jesus represent the groups that made up the Sanhedrin, the highest Jewish civil and religious court. The question is thus probably to be understood as an interrogation by a deputation from the high court, not as a matter of passing curiosity. That it would have been more appropriately posed during, or immediately after, the purging rather than a day later (verses 19, 20) is further indication that Mark was responsible for bracketing the story of the Temple with that of the fig tree. The collection of five stories of conflict between Jesus and various religious authorities (cf. 2:1 to 3:6 for a similar group) which this episode begins may originally have been attached directly to the story of the cleansing, showing the reaction of various groups to that act.

The question posed in verse 30 ("from heaven" means "from God") by Jesus shows how closely Jesus and John were identified. What was said about the authority of the one would be true about the authority of the other. That is the dilemma the question posed for the Sanhedrin deputation. They must have wanted to answer: "from men"—i.e., not from God—but fear of the crowd made that answer impossible. Their unwillingness to answer also shows they have not understood the meaning of Jesus' activity in the Temple as Mark interpreted it (verses 22–25) and thus were unable to come to Jesus in faith (verse 22). Only those who approach Jesus in faith are able to understand his authority.

STUDY QUESTION: What is there about Jesus' authority that makes it understandable only to those who come to him in faith?

12:1–12
Jesus challenges the Temple authorities

¹ 12 He went on to speak to them in parables.
"A man planted a vineyard; he fenced it
around, dug out a trough for the winepress and
built a tower; then he leased it to tenants and
² went abroad. ·When the time came, he sent a
servant to the tenants to collect from them his
³ share of the produce from the vineyard. ·But
they seized the man, thrashed him and sent him
⁴ away empty-handed. ·Next he sent another servant to them; him they beat about the head and
⁵ treated shamefully. ·And he sent another and him
they killed; then a number of others, and they
⁶ thrashed some and killed the rest. ·He had still
someone left: his beloved son. He sent him to
them last of all. 'They will respect my son,' he
⁷ said. ·But those tenants said to each other, 'This
is the heir. Come on, let us kill him, and the in-
⁸ heritance will be ours.' ·So they seized him and
killed him and threw him out of the vineyard.
⁹ Now what will the owner of the vineyard do? He
will come and make an end of the tenants and
¹⁰ give the vineyard to others. ·Have you not read
this text of scripture:

It was the stone rejected by the builders
that became the keystone.
¹¹   This was the Lord's doing
and it is wonderful to see?"

¹² And they would have liked to arrest him, because they realized that the parable was aimed at
them, but they were afraid of the crowds. So
they left him alone and went away.

✠

This is the third time Mark identifies what Jesus says as "parable" (cf. 3:23; 4:2), and the second time it is directed against Jesus' opponents (as in 3:23). There is some question whether the parable in its present form can go back to Jesus. Some of the wording in verse 1 is closer to the Greek translation of Isaiah 5:1–2 than to the Hebrew original, and verse 10 is quoted directly from the Greek version of the Old Testament (the Septuagint), something Jesus, whose native language would have been Aramaic, would be less likely to do. It points to a later time in the church, when Greek had become the usual language. The present form of the story also has details that conform it to the history of Israel's relationship to God. As they rejected his prophets (here, the various servants in verses 2–5), so they rejected his Son (verses 6–8). Such allegorization of detail drawn from the completed story of Jesus is carried even further in Matthew (21:33–46) and Luke (20:9–19). Again, the quotation in verse 10 from Psalm 118:22–23 and the idea of Jesus as cornerstone were popular in early church tradition (Ac 4:11; 1 P 2:6, 7; Rm 9:33; Ep 2:20). Finally, verse 9, with its reference to God rejecting Israel and turning to "others" may well reflect the later experience of the church which found its gospel rejected by the Jewish people as a whole but given a ready hearing by gentiles. St. Paul engaged in similar reflections on Israel's rejection and the inclusion of gentiles (Rm 11:17–24). All of this shows the extent to which later tradition contributed to the present shape of the parable.

What form the parable may have had if it came from Jesus, before the experience of the church after his resurrection colored its details, is difficult to say. Much has been made of the strange reaction of the tenants to the owner's rightful claim through his servants to a portion of the harvest. Precedents have been sought in the rebellious attitudes of Jewish peasants toward absentee landlords, in order to qualify this parable as originating with Jesus. Yet aside from the fact that characters in parables do not act in accordance with "historical precedent" (e.g., the father in Lk 15:22–23; the Samaritan in Lk 10:33–35), in the present form of the parable the tenants represent the rebellious leaders of Israel. Who would claim that rebellion against a loving God is logical?

The activity of the owner of the vineyard is equally strange. Why, knowing the brutal, indeed murderous acts of the tenants against his many servants, would he then send his only son into their hands? But again, in the present story, the owner is God. Who would claim that forgiving love (i.e., grace) is a "logical' response to human rebellion and sin?

Clearly, this parable as Mark presents it is not designed to tell a story of events that could and did happen ordinarily in Roman-occupied Palestine. It is a story of the strange, illogical relationship between rebellious Israel and its merciful God, a relationship that will now be shown, in the story of Jesus' passion, at its illogical, rebellious worst and its triumphant, gracious best. In this one story, Mark has presented in capsule form the story of the relationship between God, Israel, and the church, and that is the way we ought to read it.

STUDY QUESTION: Why would Mark have thought this was an appropriate place to put this parable?

12:13–17
What about taxes?

13   Next they sent to him some Pharisees and some
14 Herodians to catch him out in what he said. ·These
      came and said to him, "Master, we know you are
      an honest man, that you are not afraid of anyone,
      because a man's rank means nothing to you, and
      that you teach the way of God in all honesty. Is
      it permissible to pay taxes to Caesar or not?
15 Should we pay, yes or no?" ·Seeing through their
      hypocrisy he said to them, "Why do you set this
      trap for me? Hand me a denarius and let me see
16 it." ·They handed him one and he said, "Whose
      head is this? Whose name?" "Caesar's," they told
17 him. ·Jesus said to them, "Give back to Caesar
      what belongs to Caesar—and to God what belongs
      to God." This reply took them completely by
      surprise.

✠

Apparently sent by the Sanhedrin (on "they" in
verse 13, see note on 11:27), representatives of two
Jewish groups come to lay a trap for Jesus. Pharisees
sought to take on themselves as laymen priestly rules of
purity to fulfill literally Exodus 19:6. Herodians (only
otherwise mentioned in 3:6) are an unknown group,
perhaps supporters of the line of the Roman puppet
Herod the Great. Their compliments are meant to force
Jesus, as acknowledged teacher, to answer their trick
question. The tax was probably the Roman head tax,
whose institution in Palestine in A.D. 6 led to a small

revolt (cf. Ac 5:37). It continued to be opposed by zealous Jewish nationalists: how could a people whose king was God pay tribute to any earthly sovereign? The question (verse 14) was designed to show Jesus either a traitor to Rome (don't pay their taxes) or to the Jews (do pay them).

Jesus, recognizing that intention, asked to see a silver Roman coin, equivalent in value to one twelve-hour day's labor (cf. Mt 20:2, 6, 12). Jesus' answer (verse 17) is more revealing in the Greek, where Jesus asks whose "image" is on the coin. That would immediately call to his listeners' mind the verse in Genesis (1:26) which says God made man "in his own image." Thus, Jesus says, an item belongs to the one whose image it bears. Coins can go to Caesar, but a human being, bearing the image of God, can only have him as true master.

STUDY QUESTION: Where do we draw the line to determine when demands of the state infringe on a loyalty we can give only to God?

12:18–27
Riddles on the resurrection

18 Then some Sadducees—who deny that there is a resurrection—came to him and they put this
19 question to him, ·"Master, we have it from Moses in writing, if a man's brother dies leaving a wife but no child, the man must marry the widow to
20 raise up children for his brother. ·Now there

were seven brothers. The first married a wife and
21 then died leaving no children. ·The second married the widow, and he too died leaving no chil-
22 dren; with the third it was the same, ·and none of
the seven left any children. Last of all the woman
23 herself died. ·Now at the resurrection, when they
rise again, whose wife will she be, since she had
been married to all seven?"

24   Jesus said to them, "Is not the reason why you
go wrong, that you understand neither the scrip-
25 tures nor the power of God? ·For when they rise
from the dead, men and women do not marry; no,
26 they are like the angels in heaven. ·Now about the
dead rising again, have you never read in the Book
of Moses, in the passage about the Bush, how
God spoke to him and said: I am the God of
Abraham, the God of Isaac and the God of Jacob?
27 He is God, not of the dead, but of the living. You
are very much mistaken."

✠

One after another, religious authorities come forth to
contest Jesus. This is the only mention of Sadducees in
Mark's Gospel. An aristocratic group of priestly families from whom the high priest was chosen, Sadducees
regarded as normative Scripture only the first five
books of the Old Testament (the Pentateuch). Since
the only references to resurrection in the Old Testament—and they are scarce indeed—appear in later
writings (Is 26:19; Dn 12:2; perhaps also Jb
19:25–26; Ps 73:23–24; Is 25:8), the Sadducees denied such an idea (cf. Ac 23:6–8; it was a bone of con-
tention between Pharisees and Sadducees). The question they put to Jesus, based on the law of "levirate
marriage" (Dt 25:5–10), was designed to show the ab-
surd consequences of belief in resurrection. Obviously,

if (as they thought) Moses had written such a law about marriage, he could not have known of a resurrection. Otherwise he would have foreseen just such difficulties as these, and would not have prescribed such marriage practices.

Jesus' answer is twofold. The first (verses 24–25) contests the supposition in the question that the state of the risen will be similar to that of our world in all respects. Since the absurdity of the question presupposed such continuity, Jesus' denial of that continuity (the risen, like the angels, live in different relationships to one another than we do in our present world) renders the example pointless. Jesus here employs ideas already widespread in certain circles of Judaism (cf. Tb 12:19, where the angel Raphael notes that he does not eat).

Jesus' second answer is taken from Scripture the Sadducees must acknowledge (Ex 3:6). The logic seems to be that since God says he is (not, he was) the God of Abraham, Isaac, and Jacob, they must still be alive, perhaps in some risen state. The further statement, recalling the reference to God's power in verse 24, makes clear that the power of the living God is too great to be overcome by death. If God was powerful enough to create life in the beginning, he is powerful enough to recreate it after death. That is the point the Sadducees have missed in their speculative attempts to set limits on God's power.

STUDY QUESTION: Does this passage mean that all speculation about the conditions of life after death is pointless?

12:28–34
Above all, love

28   One of the scribes who had listened to them
debating and had observed how well Jesus had
answered them, now came up and put a question
to him, "Which is the first of all the command-
29   ments?" ·Jesus replied, "This is the first: Listen,
30   Israel, the Lord our God is the one Lord, ·and
you must love the Lord your God with all your
heart, with all your soul, with all your mind and
31   with all your strength. ·The second is this: You
must love your neighbor as yourself. There is no
32   commandment greater than these." ·The scribe
said to him, "Well spoken, Master; what you have
said is true: that he is one and there is no other.
33   To love him with all your heart, with all your understanding and strength, and to love your neighbor as yourself, this is far more important than
34   any holocaust or sacrifice." ·Jesus, seeing how
wisely he had spoken, said, "You are not far from
the kingdom of God." And after that no one dared
to question him any more.

☨

This is the only story in Mark's Gospel where a
scribe has a positive attitude to Jesus. It indicates that,
contrary to the usual view, not all orthodox Jews rejected Jesus.

Well-known rabbis were occasionally asked the question here put to Jesus. The ability to state in succinct
form the basis of the law was honored as an indication

of legal expertise. Jesus' answer is drawn from Jewish Scripture. Verses 29–30 are part of a statement of faith every adult Jewish male was expected to recite daily. The second part of the answer (verse 31) qualifies the first. One cannot love God unless that love is made real toward one's fellow human beings. There is some evidence that these two commands had been combined prior to Jesus and identified as central to the law. What is important is not that Jesus said them, but rather that he incorporated them into his own life, by accepting as fellow human beings people whom others despised (cf. 2:16; 10:14), and by obeying God's will right up to a cross.

The scribe's response, especially his added remark about sacrifices (verse 33; he had prophetic precedent —e.g., Is 1:11; Ho 6:6), shows that he understood the command not as a basis for deducing the remainder of the law as logical extensions, but as a command so important that its observance rendered all other laws superfluous.

However we may want to understand Jesus' final remark about the scribe's relation to God's kingdom (is the kingdom about to come? is it present already? is it where Jesus is?), the stunning fact is that Jesus could make such a statement. Who can really say such a thing except God himself? Perhaps that is why, after that saying, "no one dared to question him any more."

STUDY QUESTION: Where else in Mark's Gospel has Jesus done or said things which could normally be expected only from God?

12:35-37
A puzzle about David's son

35   Later, while teaching in the Temple, Jesus said,
      "How can the scribes maintain that the Christ is
36 the son of David? ·David himself, moved by the
    Holy Spirit, said:

> The Lord said to my Lord:
> Sit at my right hand
> and I will put your enemies
> under your feet.

37 David himself calls him Lord, in what way then
    can he be his son?" And the great majority of the
    people heard this with delight.

✠

This passage represents an unsolved problem in interpreting Mark. The clear intention of the verses is
simply that the Messiah is not of Davidic descent. If
David can say (verse 36): "The Lord [i.e., God] said
to *my* Lord [i.e., the Messiah], sit . . ." (Ps 110:1),
and if in Jewish custom no one would address his own
descendant as "Lord," then when David does call the
Messiah "Lord," it demonstrates that David could not
be speaking to his descendant. Could Mark have
thought Jesus was not from David's line? Nowhere in
this Gospel is Jesus associated with Bethlehem, the
"city of David" (cf. Lk 2:11), nor is Jesus identified as
David's son in the entry into Jerusalem (cf. Mt 21:9).
Only blind Bartimaeus calls him that, and the title is of

no significance for that story (it may only have been another term for "Jew"; cf. Mk 11:10, where apparently any Jew could claim David as "father"). In its present position, the passage continues to demonstrate Jesus' superiority over the religious questions and doctrines of official Judaism, but its meaning is a puzzle in light of the early and regular New Testament witness to Jesus as David's descendant.

STUDY QUESTION: Some have suggested this passage means Jesus as true Messiah is very different from Jewish expectations expressed in the phrase "son of David." What do you think?

12:38–44
Spiritual pride and a generous widow

38 In his teaching he said, "Beware of the scribes who like to walk about in long robes, to be greeted
39 obsequiously in the market squares, ·to take the front seats in the synagogues and the places of
40 honor at banquets; ·these are the men who swallow the property of widows, while making a show of lengthy prayers. The more severe will be the sentence they receive."
41 He sat down opposite the treasury and watched the people putting money into the treasury, and
42 many of the rich put in a great deal. ·A poor widow came and put in two small coins, the equiv-
43 alent of a penny. ·Then he called his disciples and said to them, "I tell you solemnly, this poor widow has put more in than all who have contributed to

⁴⁴ the treasury; ·for they have all put in money they had over, but she from the little she had has put in everything she possessed, all she had to live on."

✠

These two stories may have been associated with one another, and with the one preceding them, because of catchword similarity: scribe (verses 35 and 38) and widow (verses 40 and 42). The fact that the second story (verses 41–44) presumes routine continuation of Temple activities indicates it originated apart from the present context. As they now stand, these two passages report the final episodes of Jesus' public ministry.

Not all scribes are condemned by Jesus in these verses (cf. 12:34). His words are directed against those characterized by an illusory practice of piety that masks an impious reality. "Long robes" were to be worn at prayer and other times of scribal duties (verse 38; for a similar point, cf. Mt 23:5). In the market place their only function would be self-glorification. Since the superior first received the greeting of an inferior before returning it, pretentious people sought to be greeted first ("obsequiously" is not in the Greek; the same word for "greeting" is used in Lk 1:29, 41; 1 Co 16:21). Piety for show was also condemned in contemporary Judaism.

The story of the widow's tiny but generous offering has parallels in both Jewish and pagan writings of Jesus' time. The "treasury" probably refers to the thirteen trumpet-shaped receptacles that were placed around an outer court of the Temple (Court of the Israelite Women). The story of one who "gave her all" is a fitting transition to the story of the passion, where Jesus will give himself for us.

STUDY QUESTION: Why would Jesus say those who pretend to piety will receive harsher judgment than those who do not cover evil deeds with such a cloak (verse 40)?

Mark 13:1–37
ON EVENTS BEFORE THE END

13:1–13
Signs of distress: tumult and division

¹ 13 As he was leaving the Temple one of his disciples said to him, "Look at the size of those stones, Master! Look at the size of those ² buildings!" ·And Jesus said to him, "You see these great buildings? Not a single stone will be left on another: everything will be destroyed."

³ And while he was sitting facing the Temple, on the Mount of Olives, Peter, James, John and An-
⁴ drew questioned him privately, ·"Tell us when is this going to happen and what sign will there be that all this is about to be fulfilled?"

⁵ Then Jesus began to tell them, "Take care that ⁶ no one deceives you. ·Many will come using my my name and saying, 'I am he,' and they will de-
⁷ ceive many. ·When you hear of wars and rumors of wars, do not be alarmed, this is something that ⁸ must happen, but the end will not be yet. ·For nation will fight against nation, and kingdom against kingdom. There will be earthquakes here and there; there will be famines. This is the beginning of the birth pangs.

⁹ "Be on your guard: they will hand you over to sanhedrins; you will be beaten in synagogues; and you will stand before governors and kings for my ¹⁰ sake, to bear witness before them, ·since the Good News must first be proclaimed to all the nations.

11   "And when they lead you away to hand you
      over, do not worry beforehand about what to say;
      no, say whatever is given to you when the time
      comes, because it is not you who will be speak-
12   ing: it will be the Holy Spirit. ·Brother will betray
      brother to death, and the father his child; chil-
      dren will rise against their parents and have them
13   put to death. ·You will be hated by all men on
      account of my name; but the man who stands firm
      to the end will be saved."

☩

Mark 13 has often been called the "little apocalypse." An apocalypse is a kind of literature designed
to comfort readers in a period of great distress by as-
suring them that that period is part of God's plan for
history, and by revealing to them ("apocalypse" comes
from a Greek word meaning "revelation") what events
must yet occur before present tribulations end. What
the disciples ask in verse 4 is what an apocalypse seeks
to answer. This type of literature was popular in Jewish
and early Christian circles. Of the many apocalypses
written, two were included in our Bible, Daniel in the
Old Testament, and the Apocalypse of John in the New
Testament.

This chapter also serves as Jesus' farewell discourse,
a device familiar in the literature of biblical times. Before his death, a famous figure would give a last speech
which contained his final testimony (for Jesus, cf. also
Jn 14 to 17; for Moses, Dt 31:28 to 32:52; for David, 1
Ch 28:1 to 29:5, to mention only a few). Mark 13
contains the longest speech Jesus gives in Mark, and it
concludes the material dealing with the Temple.

The first five verses are Mark's introduction to these
traditions, and they contain familiar Markan ideas (pri-

vate instruction to disciples; cf. 4:10; 7:17; 9:28; 10:10) and language. Although what follows purports to refer to the destruction of the Temple (verses 1–2), its scope is obviously far wider. Perhaps the actual destruction of the Temple in Jerusalem by the Romans in A.D. 70 led some Christians to think that was the sign of the end, and Mark used Jesus' prophecy of its destruction to warn that that was not the case. That is clearly the point of verses 6–10. Christians are not to let themselves be deceived by statements that the end is near simply because someone announces it in Christ's name (verses 5–6). The signs of civil strife are preliminary; the final signs are cosmic and could hardly be misinterpreted (cf. verses 24–27).

Verses 9–13 probably reflect the experience of early Christians who were persecuted for their faith. In fact, Matthew put these verses into the framework of Jesus' instructions to the disciples as they prepared their first preaching mission (Mt 10:17–22). Two points are made about such suffering. First, despite all appearances, God has not deserted them. In critical moments, his Spirit will aid them, and help them give appropriate testimony (verse 11). Second, such testimony is precisely the purpose of that persecution. It gives Christians a chance to tell of Christ to people they otherwise would never confront (e.g., governors and kings, verse 9), and helps fulfill God's plan of having the gospel proclaimed worldwide (verse 10).

That in such circumstances families will be disrupted (verse 13) should not be surprising, especially in light of what Jesus said about putting loyalty to him above all family ties (cf. Mt 10:35–36; Lk 12:52–53). Yet even this must be borne for the sake of following Jesus

(cf. 8:34), and those who do hold fast to him to the
end he will not desert.

STUDY QUESTION: How seriously ought we take someone who, claiming the authority of
the Bible, interprets some events to
mean the end of the world is at
hand?

13:14–27
Be careful of false interpretations
of the times

14   "When you see the disastrous abomination set
up where it ought not to be (let the reader understand), then those in Judaea must escape to the
15 mountains; ·if a man is on the housetop, he must
not come down to go into the house to collect any
16 of his belongings; ·if a man is in the fields, he
17 must not turn back to fetch his cloak. ·Alas for
those with child, or with babies at the breast,
18 when those days come! ·Pray that this may not
19 be in winter. ·For in those days there will be such
distress as, until now, has not been equaled since
the beginning when God created the world, nor
20 ever will be again. ·And if the Lord had not short-
ened that time, no one would have survived; but
he did shorten the time, for the sake of the elect
whom he chose.
21   "And if anyone says to you then, 'Look, here
is the Christ' or, 'Look, he is there,' do not be-
22 lieve it; ·for false Christs and false prophets will
arise and produce signs and portents to deceive
23 the elect, if that were possible. ·You therefore

must be on your guard. I have forewarned you of
everything.
24   "But in those days, after that time of distress,
the sun will be darkened, the moon will lose
25 its brightness, ·the stars will come falling from
heaven and the powers in the heavens will be
26 shaken. ·And then they will see the Son of Man
coming in the clouds with great power and glory;
27 then too he will send the angels to gather his
chosen from the four winds, from the ends of the
world to the ends of heaven."

☩

These verses present us with a strange tension between descriptions of events that will let us know when
the end will come upon us (verses 14-20), and a warning that such an interpretation of those events is decep-
tive (verses 21-23). It almost looks as though verses
21-23 want to warn the reader that any attempt to
forecast the events preceding Christ's second appearance is doomed to failure. The fact that verses 14-20
are bracketed by warnings about false Christs (verses
5-6, 21-23) strengthens that impression. St. Paul
faced similar problems with people who thought they
could forecast end times (2 Th 2).
The events described in verses 14-20 occur in a
specific locality, namely Judaea. As in the writings of
Old Testament prophets, local events are here understood to have worldwide significance. Perhaps Mark
has taken a Christian prophetic writing and put it here,
bracketed by warnings that the end is not yet at hand.
The meaning of the "disastrous abomination" (a
phrase taken from Daniel 11:21, where it referred to a
desecration of the Jerusalem Temple in 167 B.C.; cf.
also Dt 9:27; 12:11), which in verse 14 is the event

which will tell one when to flee, is unknown. Luke interpreted it to mean the fall of Jerusalem (Lk 21:20). If the material in verses 14–20 was written when Mark got it (the reference to the "reader" in verse 14 would bear that out), it could refer to the attempt by the Roman emperor Caligula to have his statue erected in the Jerusalem Temple in A.D. 40, something which, had it occurred, Jews would have regarded as a Temple desecration. We are not sure, however, to what the phrase refers.

Flat-roofed Palestinian houses are presumed (verse 15), with an outside staircase giving access. The heavier cloak was laid aside for work in the fields (verse 16). The point is that any delay in flight, however trivial, will be fatal, so suddenly does the danger come. Pregnant and nursing women are at a disadvantage in such situations, and winter would mean no food could be found in the wild. The "great tribulations" (cf. Dn 12:1) are perhaps the "messianic woes," in Jewish tradition a period of increasing suffering which would precede rescue by the returning Messiah. Verse 20 assumes God has a timetable for the duration of the suffering which, if held to, would mean no one could survive to the end (cf. verse 13). God mercifully shortens the period of suffering, however, thus allowing some at least to hold fast to the end.

To think all this lets one predict when Christ will return is wrong, however (verses 21–22), and those who think so will be deceived (cf. 2 Th 2:9, where such deception is attributed to Satan). Only after that distress is over, and unmistakable cosmic signs occur (verses 24–25; cf. Is 13:10; 34:4) will the Son of Man (i.e., Christ) come in an unmistakable way (cf. Dn 7:13).

Only then will the angels assemble God's chosen ones to live in his kingdom.

Mark seems to want to do two things here. First, he wants to make clear that when Christ returns, it will fulfill the many Old Testament prophecies about the end, as shown by the many places the language of these verses reflects Old Testament passages. Second, Mark wants to warn his readers not to think they can anticipate when that fulfillment will take place by a cleverly calculated interpretation of certain preliminary events. When that end is at hand, no one can miss it. Before it comes, no one can predict it. The point of these verses is to put us on guard against those who attempt such predictions (verse 23).

STUDY QUESTION: Is it important to know what the "disastrous abomination" was to understand the point Mark wants to make in these verses?

13:28–37
In uncertain times, stay alert!

28 "Take the fig tree as a parable: as soon as its twigs grow supple and its leaves come out, you
29 know that summer is near. ·So with you when you see these things happening: know that he is near,
30 at the very gates. ·I tell you solemnly, before this generation has passed away all these things will
31 have taken place. ·Heaven and earth will pass away, but my words will not pass away.
32 "But as for that day or hour, nobody knows

it, neither the angels of heaven, nor the Son; no
one but the Father.

³³   "Be on your guard, stay awake, because you
³⁴ never know when the time will come. ·It is like a
man traveling abroad: he has gone from home,
and left his servants in charge, each with his own
task; and he has told the doorkeeper to stay
³⁵ awake. ·So stay awake, because you do not know
when the master of the house is coming, evening,
³⁶ midnight, cockcrow, dawn; ·if he comes unex-
³⁷ pectedly he must not find you asleep. ·And what
I say to you I say to all: Stay awake!"

✠

We find in this passage the same tension we found in
the preceding one. Verses 28–30 presume that certain
events presage the coming end (cf. verses 14–20),
while verses 32–36 say such information is unavailable
(cf. verses 21–23). The problem is heightened by the
phrase "these things happening" in verse 29. "These
things" cannot refer to the events described in verses
24–27. There the end is not near, it is present. It could
best refer to what is described in verses 14–20. Perhaps
in its pre-Markan form, verses 14–20 and 28–31 were
connected into a kind of apocalyptic guide for reckoning when the end was coming. Mark corrected that
view by inserting the qualifications we find in verses
21–23, and especially in verse 32.

Verse 28 is similar to other sayings of Jesus (e.g., Lk
12:54–56), where Jesus' own activity is a sign that
God's future has cast its shadow on the present through
the words and acts of Jesus. But that is a far cry from
the kind of apocalyptic reckoning that tries to pinpoint
the date of the arrival of that future. Mark in this chapter may be attempting to recover for these and similar

words of Jesus, embedded in this prior tradition, a context closer to that expressed by Jesus himself. For Jesus, the coming of that future meant: prepare while there is time. Be ready (cf. 1:15). That of course is the point Mark is trying to make, especially with verses 33–36, sayings which again reflect other words of Jesus we have (e.g., Lk 12:35–40).

Verses 30 and 31 may also be original words of Jesus, with verse 30 similar to Mark 9:1, and verse 31 applying to Jesus' own words what in another context he applied to words of the law (Mt 5:18). The two verses are apparently linked by catchword association, with "these things" linking verses 29 and 30, and "pass away" linking verses 30 and 31. Perhaps in such a way the pre-Markan tradition formed an apocalyptic tract from words of Jesus.

Whatever the origin of this material may have been, however, what Mark wants to say to us is clear enough. Until Jesus comes—and Mark never doubted that he would—the only appropriate posture for Christians is watchful waiting (verses 33–37). It can hardly be accidental that he chose just this emphasis to conclude this section. It is apparently the purpose for which Mark composed this whole chapter.

STUDY QUESTIONS: What kind of circumstances would make such a warning to "stay awake" appropriate? Jesus' delayed return? Persecution for their faith? Is the warning still appropriate for us?

Mark 14:1–42
THE FINAL ACTS OF JESUS

14:1–11
Jesus prepared for the cross:
a woman and a traitor

¹ **14** It was two days before the Passover and the feast of Unleavened Bread, and the chief priests and the scribes were looking for a way to arrest Jesus by some trick and have him ² put to death. ·For they said, "It must not be during the festivities, or there will be a disturbance among the people."

³ Jesus was at Bethany in the house of Simon the leper; he was at dinner when a woman came in with an alabaster jar of very costly ointment, pure nard. She broke the jar and poured the oint⁴ ment on his head. ·Some who were there said to one another indignantly, "Why this waste of oint⁵ ment? ·Ointment like this could have been sold for over three hundred denarii and the money given to the poor"; and they were angry with her. ⁶ But Jesus said, "Leave her alone. Why are you upsetting her? What she has done for me is one ⁷ of the good works. ·You have the poor with you always, and you can be kind to them whenever ⁸ you wish, but you will not always have me. ·She has done what was in her power to do: she has ⁹ anointed my body beforehand for its burial. ·I tell you solemnly, wherever throughout all the world

the Good News is proclaimed, what she has done
will be told also, in remembrance of her."
10   Judas Iscariot, one of the Twelve, approached
the chief priests with an offer to hand Jesus over
11   to them. ·They were delighted to hear it, and
promised to give him money; and he looked for
a way of betraying him when the opportunity
should occur.

☩

Mark chose to introduce his narrative of Jesus' passion with an account of an anointing of Jesus which he
found in his tradition. Both Luke (7:36–50) and John
(12:1–8) knew it in somewhat varied form, and put it
in different contexts. In characteristic fashion, Mark
bracketed that account with another tradition, this one
about Jesus' betrayal by Judas. It shows Mark continued to arrange and shape his traditions in this part of
his narrative as he did in the earlier parts.

Simon the Leper (verse 3) is mentioned only here in
Mark, so we know nothing further about him. Nor is
the woman who anointed Jesus named. Only much
later was she identified with Mary Magdalene. Her
great sacrifice (the cost of the ointment was about a
year's wage for a laborer) points to the importance of
Jesus. That is emphasized in verse 9, where what she
did is remembered rather than who she was. What she
did was, in an act of prophetic anticipation, to anoint
the body of Jesus. It was the only such anointing he
would receive. Before his corpse could be anointed
later, he had risen from the grave (cf. 16:1–6).

Verse 7 has often been distorted. It does not forbid
help to the poor, and it is surely no command to shape
an economic system in such a way that some people are

held in poverty. Since we cannot anoint the body of
Jesus, our responsibility is to the poor (cf. Mt
25:34–46). As so often in Mark, those around Jesus
fail to understand the importance of the events of
which they are a part. Here again, they failed to understand this further announcement of Jesus' impending
death, preoccupied as they were with their own concerns.

Mark gives no indication of what it was Judas betrayed (verse 11). Perhaps, in light of the authorities'
desire not to arouse the wrath of the crowds with a
public arrest (verse 2; cf. 11:32; 12:12), Judas arranged to tell them when and where they might arrest
Jesus in secret, but that is only guesswork. Nor does
Mark give any motivation for Judas' act. That he did
not do it for the money is clear from the fact that pay-
ment is mentioned (verse 11) only after Judas arranged the betrayal (verse 10). Only later is that mo-
tive introduced (Mt 26:15) and then expanded (Jn
12:4–6). What is clear is that the hour of Jesus' death,
so often announced (3:6; 8:32; 9:31; 10:33–34;
12:12) is now at hand. With these verses, we begin the
climax of Mark's narrative.

STUDY QUESTIONS: What does Mark want to tell us by
combining these two stories? How
do they complement one another?
What contrasts are apparent?

14:12–16
Passover preparations

12   On the first day of Unleavened Bread, when the
      Passover lamb was sacrificed, his disciples said to
      him, "Where do you want us to go and make the
13   preparations for you to eat the passover?" ·So he
      sent two of his disciples, saying to them, "Go
      into the city and you will meet a man carrying a
14   pitcher of water. Follow him, ·and say to the
      owner of the house which he enters, 'The Mas-
      ter says: Where is my dining room in which I can
15   eat the passover with my disciples?' ·He will show
      you a large upper room furnished with couches,
      all prepared. Make the preparations for us
16   there." ·The disciples set out and went to the city
      and found everything as he had told them, and
      prepared the passover.

✠

These verses, like 11:1–5, presume more frequent
visits and wider acquaintance with Jerusalem by Jesus
than the present outline of Mark indicates. That shows
this was again an independent tradition, which Mark
has used to set forward his story of the passion. It is
the only passage in Mark that identifies Jesus' last meal
with his disciples as a Passover meal.

The Passover, which celebrated the escape of the
Jews from Egyptian bondage, had early been combined
with a second feast, that of Unleavened Bread (Dt
16:2–3). There is some evidence that the day of prepa-

ration which began the festival was also identified as
the first day of Unleavened Bread. The day of preparation, when the Passover lamb was slaughtered in the
Temple, was followed by the celebration of the Passover meal, during which the lamb was eaten. Since
Jews reckoned days as ending and beginning at sunset,
not at midnight as we do, the day of preparation ended
at sunset, and the Passover began. Thus a lamb sac-
rificed in the afternoon, before sunset (day of preparation), would be eaten that evening, after sunset (Passover). It is this time scheme that is presumed in these
verses, where preparations were made during the day
for the Passover meal that evening.

14:17–31
Eucharist in the midst of disciples' failure

17   When evening came he arrived with the Twelve.
18 And while they were at table eating, Jesus said,
      "I tell you solemnly, one of you is about to betray
19 me, one of you eating with me." ·They were dis-
      tressed and asked him, one after another, "Not I,
20 surely?" ·He said to them, "It is one of the Twelve,
      one who is dipping into the same dish with me.
21 Yes, the Son of Man is going to his fate, as the
      scriptures say he will, but alas for that man by
      whom the Son of Man is betrayed! Better for that
      man if he had never been born!"
22   And as they were eating he took some bread,
      and when he had said the blessing he broke it and
      gave it to them. "Take it," he said, "this is my
23 body." ·Then he took a cup, and when he had re-
      turned thanks he gave it to them, and all drank

24 from it, ·and he said to them, "This is my blood,
   the blood of the covenant, which is to be poured
25 out for many. ·I tell you solemnly, I shall not
   drink any more wine until the day I drink the new
   wine in the kingdom of God."
26   After psalms had been sung they left for the
27 Mount of Olives. ·And Jesus said to them, "You
   will all lose faith, for the scripture says: I shall
   strike the shepherd and the sheep will be scat-
28 tered, ·however after my resurrection I shall go
29 before you to Galilee." ·Peter said, "Even if all
30 lose faith, I will not." ·And Jesus said to him, "I
   tell you solemnly, this day, this very night, before
   the cock crows twice, you will have disowned me
31 three times." ·But he repeated still more earnestly,
   "If I have to die with you, I will never disown
   you." And they all said the same.

☩

As was the case with 14:1–11, these verses have
been assembled by Mark from his traditions. He has
again used his familiar bracketing technique, this time
bracketing the story of the institution of the Eucharist
with traditions about the betrayal of Jesus, both by
Judas (verses 17–21) and by Peter and the other disciples (verses 27–31). In that way, the saving death of
Jesus is placed in starkest contrast to the faithlessness
of his closest followers.

The frequent allusions to Old Testament passages
(in verse 18 to Ps 41:9; in verse 21 to "scriptures"; in
verse 27 to Zc 13:7) show that Jesus' death was not an
unfortunate accident but was part of God's plan for our
salvation. Yet that plan cannot be used as an excuse to
evade responsibility for one's own acts, as verse 21
makes clear. Within the framework of God's saving plan

for humankind, we remain free, responsible people. No plea of historical necessity will allow the disciples, or us, to excuse the betrayal of Jesus.

These verses also present the contrast between what the disciples said and what they would eventually do. While there was as yet only one traitor in the formal sense (verses 10–11), before this night was out, all had shown their solidarity with Judas in betraying their Lord (cf. especially verse 31 with verses 50, 66–72). The confident assurance that they were not traitors ("Not I, surely," verse 19) and the brave claims of Peter, which they all repeated (verses 29–31), show up in starkest contrast to their eventual acts.

There is nothing in the description of the meal (verses 22–24) that would make it anything more than a normal Jewish meal. There is nothing in the description that would compel us to understand it as a Passover celebration. The repetition of the phrase about eating (verse 22) probably shows verses 22–25 once circulated independently of the present context. So does the reference to breaking bread, an act that began a meal. It would more properly have been reported in verse 18 if these verses had originated in their present order.

The description of the meal was already at the time of Mark part of the eucharistic liturgy, as 1 Corinthians 11:23–25 show. Theological reflection on the meaning of this event produced varying descriptions of it in the New Testament (cf. Mt 26:26–29; Lk 22:15–20; 1 Co 11:23–25; Jn 6:35–58, in addition to Mk 14:22–25) and continued to bring about changes in subsequent periods of the church's history. Indeed, that process has continued right down to our own day! Similarly, the order in verses 23–24 (first the wine was drunk, only

then the word of institution) has for liturgical and theological reasons been reversed in the church's eucharistic
celebration (cf. already Mt 26:27). These verses, with
the implication of drinking blood, would have been all
but impossible for Jews like Jesus and the disciples (cf.
Lk 17:12; Ac 15:20, 29). They probably reflect the liturgical forms of the gentile churches. That the shed-
ding of Christ's blood instituted a new covenant would
be familiar to Jews, however (cf. Ex 24:5–8), and may
reflect an earlier stage of liturgical understanding. Finally, as verse 25 shows, the Eucharist anticipates the
return of Christ, when he will preside visibly at the
banquet for his followers in God's kingdom.

In all of this, Mark has made it clear enough that
faithfulness to Jesus requires more than brave resolve
and courageous words. In fact, it requires more than
human beings can summon forth. Any true fellowship
with Christ depends on God's grace, not human
strength. In Mark's view, the Eucharist provides a con-
tinual reminder of that fact.

STUDY QUESTIONS: To what extent do you think Mark
                    intended the disciples to stand for
                    all humanity in their reactions to
                    Jesus? If Peter speaks for them,
                    does he speak for us, too?

14:32–42
Prayer in Gethsemane:
foreboding and resolution

32 They came to a small estate called Gethsemane, and Jesus said to his disciples, "Stay here while 33 I pray." ·Then he took Peter and James and John with him. And a sudden fear came over him, and 34 great distress. ·And he said to them, "My soul is sorrowful to the point of death. Wait here, and 35 keep awake." ·And going on a little further he threw himself on the ground and prayed that, if it were possible, this hour might pass him by. 36 "Abba (Father)!" he said. "Everything is possible for you. Take this cup away from me. But 37 let it be as you, not I, would have it." ·He came back and found them sleeping, and he said to Peter, "Simon, are you asleep? Had you not the 38 strength to keep awake one hour? ·You should be awake, and praying not to be put to the test. 39 The spirit is willing, but the flesh is weak." ·Again he went away and prayed, saying the same words. 40 And once more he came back and found them sleeping, their eyes were so heavy; and they could 41 find no answer for him. ·He came back a third time and said to them, "You can sleep on now and take your rest. It is all over. The hour has come. Now the Son of Man is to be betrayed into 42 the hands of sinners. ·Get up! Let us go! My betrayer is close at hand already."

✠

This is a difficult passage to evaluate. Despite the assurance of later tradition, we do not know the location of a "Gethsemane." The story itself shows some literary confusion. It has a double introduction in verses 32 and 33–34. In verse 34 the three are told merely to stay awake, while in verse 38 they are chided for not being awake and praying. Verse 36 simply repeats what we know from verse 35, and if Jesus prayed at some distance from disciples who were sleeping, who heard what he prayed so they could record it? Such evidence makes it unlikely that we have here the record of a historical event. On the other hand, Jesus' agonized prayer prior to his death is known outside the Gospels (cf. Heb 5:7–8, probably a commentary on just this event). The word Jesus used to address God (Abba) is also found in early, nongospel traditions (cf. Rm 8:15; Ga 4:6), and surely goes back to Jesus himself. No one, Christian or Jew, used this most intimate address of the little child to its father in reference to almighty God. Calling God "Daddy" is almost as offensive to us as it was to earlier religious people. Such evidence makes it likely that this tradition is based on a historical event. This passage, like so many others in the Gospels, probably therefore reflects an event in Jesus' life (who later would invent a story that Jesus was in desperately fearful agony at the prospect of death?) which has been altered and reshaped as further theological reflection affected its telling and retelling.

Mark has placed it here to continue the contrast between brave words from the disciples (verse 31), and their actual performance (verses 37–41). The three Jesus took with him are the intimate inner circle in this Gospel (cf. 8:29; 14:29). Yet here, their unreliability is pointedly portrayed. Peter, who had been boldest in his assertion of unflinching loyalty (verse 31a), now cannot brave even one sleepless hour. James and John, who in easier times had so quickly asserted they could and would share Jesus' "cup" (10:38), join Peter in that sleep. The rejection Jesus would soon experience at the hands of "sinners" was thus prefigured by his closest friends. If Jesus fulfills God's will for him, it will not be because he was strengthened by human companionship. In the end, in his time of searing agony, the Son of Man was alone.

Despite that, Jesus withstood the temptation to abandon his God-willed course, as he had at the outset of his public ministry withstood temptation by Satan (1:13), and now prepared, he faced the final climactic events. The hour had come.

STUDY QUESTION: To what extent was Mark speaking to his own readers and their situation through this story of Jesus in Gethsemane?

JESUS IN THE HANDS OF RELIGIOUS AND CIVIL AUTHORITIES

14:43–52
Arrest and panic

43 Even while he was still speaking, Judas, one of the Twelve, came up with a number of men armed with swords and clubs, sent by the chief
44 priests and the scribes and the elders. ·Now the traitor had arranged a signal with them. "The one I kiss," he had said, "he is the man. Take him in charge, and see he is well guarded when you lead
45 him away." ·So when the traitor came, he went straight up to Jesus and said, "Rabbi!" and kissed
46 him. ·The others seized him and took him in
47 charge. ·Then one of the bystanders drew his sword and struck out at the high priest's servant, and cut off his ear.
48 Then Jesus spoke. "Am I a brigand," he said, "that you had to set out to capture me with swords
49 and clubs? ·I was among you teaching in the Temple day after day and you never laid hands on
50 me. But this is to fulfill the scriptures." ·And they
51 all deserted him and ran away. ·A young man who followed him had nothing on but a linen
52 cloth. They caught hold of him, ·but he left the cloth in their hands and ran away naked.

✠

The Markan form and language in verse 43 show us
that Mark continues to adapt individual stories from
his traditions in constructing his narrative. The reference to Jesus teaching daily in the Temple (verse 49)
is further evidence of the original independence of
these stories from their present framework. In Mark,
Jesus taught in the Temple only one day (11:27 to
13:1).

The arrest of Jesus was at the behest of the Sanhedrin (verse 43; cf. 11:27). That Jesus' betrayer was
"one of the Twelve" is firmly anchored in the oldest
traditions. Given the increasing respect shown the
Twelve in later traditions, it was hardly the invention of
a later time. The kiss with which Judas greeted Jesus
was a common form of greeting (cf. Lk 7:45; Rm
16:16; 1 Co 16:20; 1 Th 5:26; 1 P 5:14). The puzzle
is why Judas needed to identify Jesus, when his activities in the Temple would have made him familiar to
many, and why it had to be a kiss when a simple gesture would have sufficed. Perhaps it was intended to
heighten the drama of the betrayal: it was done by a
friend with a friendly gesture.

The attempt to defend Jesus (verse 47), though pa-
thetically ineffective, did catch the imagination of later
Christians. By the time Luke got the story, it was the
servant's right ear, which Jesus then healed (Lk
22:50–51), and John's tradition added that the servant
was named Malchus and the swordsman was Peter (Jn
18:10). In the light of the previous story, with Jesus'
resolve to accept his God-willed fate of suffering (cf.
14:36 with 14:41–42), such an armed mob sent to
seize him was ludicrously unnecessary.

What Scripture was fulfilled in these events (verse
49) is not clear, especially if the arrest itself, which has
just occurred, is meant. If the reference is to the fleeing

of the disciples which immediately follows (verse 50), the reference may be to Zechariah 13:7, to which Jesus had prophetically referred after the last supper with his disciples (see 14:27). The ability of the disciples to carry out their brave resolve is thus revealed to be nil. This desertion is the last act Mark reports of them in his Gospel. If they subsequently achieved authority, it would clearly not be due to such character traits as bravery or loyalty. Like all humanity, their hope lay solely in God's forgiving grace.

Who the young man was who fled naked (verses 51–52) we do not know. Neither, apparently, did Luke or Matthew, both of whom simply omit this account. All speculation on his identity is futile. His panicked flight simply emphasizes the total abandonment of Jesus to his enemies.

STUDY QUESTION: This story has little obvious theological reflection attached to it. What theological significance can you find in it?

14:53–65
Jesus before the Jewish authorities

53   They led Jesus off to the high priest; and all the chief priests and the elders and the scribes as-
54   sembled there. ·Peter had followed him at a distance, right into the high priest's palace, and was sitting with the attendants warming himself at the fire.
55   The chief priests and the whole Sanhedrin were

looking for evidence against Jesus on which they
might pass the death sentence. But they could not
⁵⁶ find any. ·Several, indeed, brought false evidence
against him, but their evidence was conflicting.
⁵⁷ Some stood up and submitted this false evidence
⁵⁸ against him, ·"We heard him say, 'I am going to
destroy this Temple made by human hands, and
in three days build another, not made by human
⁵⁹ hands.' " ·But even on this point their evidence
⁶⁰ was conflicting. ·The high priest then stood up
before the whole assembly and put this question
to Jesus, "Have you no answer to that? What is
this evidence these men are bringing against you?"
⁶¹ But he was silent and made no answer at all.
The high priest put a second question to him,
"Are you the Christ," he said, "the Son of the
⁶² Blessed One?" ·"I am," said Jesus, "and you will
see the Son of Man seated at the right hand of
the Power and coming with the clouds of heaven."
⁶³ The high priest tore his robes. "What need of wit-
⁶⁴ nesses have we now?" he said. ·"You heard the
blasphemy. What is your finding?" And they all
gave their verdict: he deserved to die.
⁶⁵   Some of them started spitting at him and, blind-
folding him, began hitting him with his fists and
shouting, "Play the prophet!" And the attendants
rained blows on him.

✠

Once again, Mark has shaped his narrative by means
of bracketing one tradition with another, this time
Jesus' "trial" with Peter's denial. Thus the resolve of
Jesus to acknowledge the truth regardless of the consequences (verses 62–64) is contrasted with Peter's total
self-denigration by denying the truth on oath (verse
71). The total abandonment of God's Son is thus displayed in all its painful reality.

An ocean of scholarly ink has been spilled in the attempt to decide whether or not the trial as Mark recorded it followed Jewish legal precedent, or whether in their zeal to destroy Jesus, the Sanhedrin trampled their own legal structures into the dust. The problem is insoluble on two grounds. One, the present account in Mark is not the kind of stenographic court report we would need for such an investigation. In its present form, it has been shaped by reflection on Old Testament passages (e.g., verse 61 by Is 53:7; Ps 38:12–13), and by later theological reflection on the meaning of Jesus' cross and resurrection. Two, we have no way of knowing what constituted normal Jewish legal procedures at this time. Old Testament practices had in many cases been modified, and new practices developed, but our only written record of them comes from the end of the second century, long after the Sanhedrin passed out of existence as a judicial body, and Jerusalem had been destroyed. Jews in first-century Palestine would hardly have known, let alone observed, all the idealized legal niceties that were set down almost two centuries later.

We can with some confidence conclude, however, that the actual sentence of execution was Roman, not Jewish, since capital punishment under ancient Jewish law was by stoning. Only Romans used the cross, and normally only on non-Roman citizens. In all likelihood, therefore, the Jews at that particular time did not have the right to carry out capital punishment. Hence, the event reflected in verses 53–64 was probably not so much a trial as a kind of preliminary hearing to secure grounds for charging Jesus before Pilate.

Mark presented this nighttime hearing as no more than an attempt to find grounds to justify a verdict long since determined (cf. 3:6; 11:18; 12:12; and 14:1 with verse 55). Mark also made clear that the charge against Jesus in regard to the Temple was false. Nowhere in Mark did Jesus say *he* would destroy the Temple (see 13:2), let alone rebuild it (this latter only in Jn 2:19). The inability of witnesses to agree on that shows clearly that, in Mark's tradition, Jesus faced trumped-up charges, and died because of them.

Jesus' answer to the second question of the high priest is Jesus' only open confession of this sort in Mark, although Jesus characteristically changes the title "Christ" to "Son of Man" (verse 62; cf. 8:29, 31). The answer is based on a combination of Psalm 110:1 and Daniel 7:13, and reflects early Christian confessional language. The point here for Mark is the contrast between who Jesus really is, and the way he is being treated. He is sentenced to die for telling the truth, and despite his true identity, he is abused and debased in most cavalier fashion (verse 65). Thus the degradation of God's Son begins, in the name of legal justice and religious rectitude.

STUDY QUESTIONS: How many contrasts can you find in this passage? What do they say about the way God confronts people, and the way people respond?

14:66-72
Peter the rock

66 While Peter was down below in the courtyard,
67 one of the high priest's servant girls came up. ·She
    saw Peter warming himself there, stared at him
    and said, "You too were with Jesus, the man from
68 Nazareth." ·But he denied it. "I do not know, I
    do not understand, what you are talking about,"
69 he said. And he went out into the forecourt. ·The
    servant girl saw him and again started telling the
70 bystanders, "This fellow is one of them." ·But
    again he denied it. A little later the bystanders
    themselves said to Peter, "You are one of them
71 for sure! Why, you are a Galilean." ·But he
    started calling down curses on himself and swear-
72 ing, "I do not know the man you speak of." ·At
    that moment the cock crew for the second time,
    and Peter recalled how Jesus had said to him,
    "Before the cock crows twice, you will have dis-
    owned me three times." And he burst into tears.

✠

In this story, we stand on the firm ground of history,
if not in the details, yet surely in the event here recited.
No one in the early church, where Peter played so important a part (e.g., Ac 2:14-36; 3:4-8; Ga 1:18),
would have invented an event like this that cast Peter
"the rock" (cf. Mk 3:16; Mt 16:18) in so negative a
light.

The details of the story may reflect the storyteller's

art. The fact that it would take a second cock-crow to remind Peter of Jesus' prophecy is all but impossible to imagine. In all subsequent accounts, only one crowing is mentioned (in Jesus' prediction and in the event: Mt 26:34, 75; Lk 22:34, 61; Jn 13:38; 18:27). Because roosters were forbidden within Jerusalem, some have suggested the original reference was to the early morning trumpet call that signaled the fourth watch of the night to the Roman garrison stationed there (it was called the *gallicinium*—literally "cock-crowing"). But the story is not dependent on such details to make its point.

Bracketing the story of Jesus' trial as it does, this account of Peter's denial of his Lord is intended to contrast the way Jesus met the question directed to him (verses 61–62) with the way Peter met the question from the servant maid. If Peter later played a leading role in Christ's church, it was not because he had earned it by his loyalty under fire. It was more likely because he was the first to whom the risen Jesus appeared (1 Co 15:15; *cephas* in Aramaic, like *petra* in Greek, means "rock"), which was understood to mean he had been forgiven (as in Jn 21:15–17, where the threefold commission corresponds to the threefold denial). Peter is thus an apostle by God's forgiving grace, not by his strength of character or moral purity.

STUDY QUESTION: What reasons would have motivated the early Christians to preserve this story about Peter?

15:1–15
Jesus before Roman authority

1 15 First thing in the morning, the chief priests together with the elders and scribes, in short the whole Sanhedrin, had their plan ready. They had Jesus bound and took him away and handed him over to Pilate.

2 Pilate questioned him, "Are you the king of the Jews?" "It is you who say it," he answered. 3 And the chief priests brought many accusations 4 against him. ·Pilate questioned him again, "Have you no reply at all? See how many accusations 5 they are bringing against you!" ·But, to Pilate's amazement, Jesus made no further reply.

6 At festival time Pilate used to release a pris- 7 oner for them, anyone they asked for. ·Now a man called Barabbas was then in prison with the rioters who had committed murder during the up- 8 rising. ·When the crowd went up and began to 9 ask Pilate the customary favor, ·Pilate answered them, "Do you want me to release for you the 10 king of the Jews?" ·For he realized it was out of jealousy that the chief priests had handed Jesus 11 over. ·The chief priests, however, had incited the crowd to demand that he should release Barabbas 12 for them instead. ·Then Pilate spoke again. "But in that case," he said to them, "what am I to do 13 with the man you call king of the Jews?" ·They 14 shouted back, "Crucify him!" ·"Why?" Pilate asked them. "What harm has he done?" But they 15 shouted all the louder, "Crucify him!" ·So Pilate, anxious to placate the crowd, released Barabbas for them and, having ordered Jesus to be scourged, handed him over to be crucified.

✠

This is no more a stenographic report of court pro-
ceedings than was the story of Jesus before the Sanhedrin. There is no hearing of evidence or questioning of
witnesses, both of which belonged to normal Roman judicial procedure. Nor is it likely that Pilate, Roman
procurator of Palestine A.D. 26–36 and infamous
among his Roman contemporaries for his corruption
and cruelty, would have engaged in dialogue with a
Jewish mob in an attempt to arrive at a verdict. As
throughout his Gospel, Mark is not so much interested
in satisfying historical curiosity as he is in pointing to
the meaning of the historical events surrounding Jesus.
He tells this story, as he tells all the others, to make
that meaning clear.

It is evident that in Mark's view it was the Jewish
Sanhedrin, not the Roman procurator, who was princi-
pally responsible for Jesus' death. Not only is the Sanhedrin again identified and its constituent groups indi-
vidually named (verse 1), but it is also clear from their
acts that they are the ones responsible for accusing
Jesus (verse 3) and for inciting the crowd to demand
his execution (verse 11). Even Pilate is pictured as seeing through their motives (verse 12). Pilate, on the
other hand, is portrayed as reluctant to condemn Jesus
(verses 4, 9, 12, 14), and as giving the Jews every opportunity to demand the release of the innocent man.
This tendency continued to operate in Christian tradition, putting more and more responsibility on the Jews
rather than the Romans for Jesus' death (cf. Mt
27:24–27 and Lk 23:13–16 for further development).
This occurred despite the undeniable fact that it was

the Romans who executed Jesus, since it was the Romans, not the Jews, who employed the cross.

The account of the release of Barabbas is also told in light of this same tendency. There is no record, Jewish or Roman, of the custom referred to in verse 6. On the other hand, an individual amnesty was always possible, and Pilate, as procurator, could have released any prisoner he chose at any time. Some such amnesty may underlie the tradition about the release of Barabbas. In its present form, however, the narrative is less concerned with Barabbas than with the point that a murderer went free and the innocent Jesus died, all at the behest of the Jewish mob incited by its leaders. It shows again where early Christians laid the blame.

Underlying this whole account, there are the deepest ironies. Jesus, silent before his accusers, fulfills Old Testament prophecy (Is 53:7; cf. 1 P 2:23), yet Pilate is oblivious to that fact (verses 4–5). Again, Jesus truly is the king of the Jews, yet not in the political sense Pilate would have meant (verse 2). At that time, any such claim would have been tantamount to rebellion against Rome. So Jesus was killed for what he in fact was, the king of God's chosen people, the Jews, yet king in a way neither the Jews nor Pilate imagined. Finally, in the episode concerning Barabbas, the supreme truth about Jesus is portrayed. Though sinless, he dies that sinners may live. Yet neither the Jews, in clamoring for Barabbas' release and Jesus' death, nor Pilate, who ultimately acceded to those requests, understood or intended the event that way.

In each instance, the actors in this historical drama are supremely unaware of the actual meaning of the events in which they participate, and which they cause

—events which, for those with eyes to see, tell the true meaning of Jesus. In such a way, says Mark, God fulfills his plan, using the acts and decisions of free human beings, even when those acts and decisions intend something quite different. Thus is God sovereign over history and over our lives, using the free acts of all humankind to fulfill his redemptive plan for all of them. That is the supreme irony of the cross, that in this event, despite the intention of the perpetrators, God saves us all.

STUDY QUESTIONS: Is there any one verse in this passage that best sums up the point Mark is making? Which one would you say it was?

15:16–20
The humiliation of the king of the Jews

16   The soldiers led him away to the inner part of the palace, that is, the Praetorium, and called the
17 whole cohort together. ·They dressed him up in purple, twisted some thorns into a crown and put
18 it on him. ·And they began saluting him, "Hail,
19 king of the Jews!" ·They struck his head with a reed and spat on him; and they went down on their
20 knees to do him homage. ·And when they had finished making fun of him, they took off the purple and dressed him in his own clothes.

☩

This event, paralleled in 14:65, shows that both Romans and Jews shared in the derision and brutal humiliation of Jesus. Similar treatment of others in Jesus' time indicates such a scene may well have occurred. Yet again, the point is the utter rejection and degrading of God's Son. The purple robe and crown, the sign of kings, was also an award for military success and political favor (cf. 1 M 10:15–20). A cohort (verse 16) consisted of between two hundred and six hundred men. Roman troops were stationed in the fortress of Antonia, adjoining the Temple complex on the north, and Pilate, in Jerusalem to keep order during Passover (procurators resided in Caesarea, to the northwest of Jerusalem), may have stayed in that fortress, or perhaps in Herod's palace.

The irony is again evident in this narrative. The soldiers, in spite of themselves, acknowledge, in both word (verse 18) and deed (verse 19b), Jesus' true identity as king of the Jews. All of this once more, unknown to the participants, fulfills Scripture (cf. Is 50:6; 53:3, 5; Ps 22:6).

STUDY QUESTION: Do you think God still accomplishes his purpose by using human acts to fulfill them, even if the humans had no intention of fulfilling God's purposes when they acted?

15:21–32

Jesus crucified and humiliated

21   They led him out to crucify him. ·They enlisted
a passer-by, Simon of Cyrene, father of Alexander
and Rufus, who was coming in from the country,
22 to carry his cross. ·They brought Jesus to the place
called Golgotha, which means the place of the
skull.
23   They offered him wine mixed with myrrh, but
24 he refused it. ·Then they crucified him, and shared
out his clothing, casting lots to decide what each
25 should get. ·It was the third hour when they cruci-
26 fied him. ·The inscription giving the charge against
27 him read: "The King of the Jews." ·And they
crucified two robbers with him, one on his right
and one on his left.
29   The passers-by jeered at him; they shook their
heads and said, "Aha! So you would destroy the
30 Temple and rebuild it in three days! ·Then save
31 yourself: come down from the cross!" ·The chief
priests and the scribes mocked him among themselves in the same way. "He saved others," they
32 said, "he cannot save himself. ·Let the Christ, the
king of Israel, come down from the cross now, for
us to see it and believe." Even those who were
crucified with him taunted him.

✠

Certain characteristics of the style and language of
this passage make it likely that Mark assembled it from
several traditions, although we can no longer follow the
process with any certainty. What is remarkable is the

simple, straightforward tone of the narrative, with no attempt to play on our sympathy for Jesus, or to arouse hate against those who destroyed him. Apparently sentimentality had no place in the telling of such a solemn event.

The condemned criminal carried the crossbar (*patibulum* in Latin) to the place of execution (verse 21). No reason is given why Simon of Cyrene (a city in North Africa) was pressed into service. Rufus and Alexander, obviously known to Mark's first readers, are as unknown to us as they were to Matthew and Luke, who omit mention of them. There is a Rufus mentioned in Romans 16:13, but the name was so common any identification is precarious. The act of offering the condemned criminal drugged wine to ease the suffering was a kindness practiced by Jews, based on Proverbs 31:6. Jesus' refusal may indicate his desire to follow God's will for his suffering to the end. We know neither where Golgotha was located nor why it was so named. As is usual in such cases, later tradition filled in the gaps.

The division of Jesus' clothing (verse 24), a practice otherwise unknown from ancient sources, may reflect the influence of Psalm 22 on the way the crucifixion was narrated (cf. Ps 22:18; cf. also Ps 22:6 with verse 20; Ps 22:16b with verse 25; 22:16a with verse 27; 22:7–8 with verse 29; 22:1 with verse 34). It is no longer possible to determine to what extent details in our story reflect history, to what extent they reflect the desire to show how this event had been prefigured in the Old Testament.

Recently discovered evidence indicates that the one crucified was at eye-level with passers-by, probably with body bent in the form of an S to keep the feet from touching the ground. The criminal was fastened to the cross by thongs or nails (the latter presumed in Jn 20:25, though nowhere explicitly stated), and death was the result of exhaustion. Thus the one crucified, with a plaque naming the crime (verse 26; cf. 15:2), served as a warning against acts Rome might consider unfriendly.

That others were crucified with Jesus may well be historical (although cf. Ps 22:16a). Their names were unknown, a gap again remedied by later traditions. As the passion story developed, they came to serve more evident theological purposes (e.g., Lk 23:39–43, where they provide opportunity for Jesus to show his forgiving love). The words of derision, implying that failure to save his own life will prove the falsity of all Jesus' claims (verses 30, 31–32a), are particularly ironic in light of God's will for Jesus, and Jesus' own words to his disciples (cf. especially 8:35). The rejection by passers-by (verse 29), religious officials (verse 31), and even those crucified with him (verse 32), all make clear the utter abandonment of God's Son as he hangs, dying, on the cross.

STUDY QUESTION: What importance do you see in understanding the story of Jesus' crucifixion in the light of Psalm 22?

15:33–39
God's Son dies

³³ When the sixth hour came there was darkness
³⁴ over the whole land until the ninth hour. ·And at
the ninth hour Jesus cried out in a loud voice,
"Eloi, Eloi, lamasabachthani?" which means, "My
³⁵ God, my God, why have you deserted me?" ·When
some of those who stood by heard this, they said,
³⁶ "Listen, he is calling on Elijah." ·Someone ran and
soaked a sponge in vinegar and, putting it on a
reed, gave it him to drink saying, "Wait and see if
³⁷ Elijah will come to take him down." ·But Jesus
³⁸ gave a loud cry and breathed his last. ·And the veil
of the Temple was torn in two from top to bottom.
³⁹ The centurion, who was standing in front of him,
had seen how he had died, and he said, "In truth
this man was a son of God."

⊬

Mark continues to toll the hours (cf. verse 25) as
they move relentlessly to the death of God's Son.
Mark's Hellenistic readers would recognize in the darkness a portent of the cosmic significance of Jesus'
death. With it, the end-time displays its first signs
(13:24; cf. Am 8:9–10).

The cry from the cross (verse 34) is the first verse of
Psalm 22. Because it is hard to imagine how anyone
who knew enough Aramaic to make sense of the cry
would confuse *eloi* with *Eliyah* (i.e., "my God" with
"Elijah"), or how anyone who understood no Aramaic

would recognize such a similarity, some have suggested
verse 34 was introduced into the tradition to interpret
Jesus' final cry (verse 37) in the light of Psalm 22, in
which so much of the passion was prefigured (see comments on verses 21–32). However that problem be re-
solved, in Mark's narrative Jesus' cry shows that now
the abandonment of God's Son is complete. Thus did
Jesus drain to its dregs his cup of suffering.

If the offer of sour wine (a better translation than
"vinegar") was historical, it was perhaps intended as a
kindly gesture of refreshment, but in Mark's tradition,
it is motivated out of curiosity. If Jesus can be kept
alive, perhaps Elijah will in fact come to save him.

The final two events give further interpretation to
Jesus' death. The Temple is desecrated (the "veil" protected the inner shrine from pollution by the world),
bringing to an end Israel's form of worship. The centurion, a gentile, confesses that Jesus is God's Son (better
than "a son of God"; the Greek is the same as Mt
14:33; 27:43; Lk 1:35), the first time an accurate title
is ascribed to Jesus intentionally (contrast verses 9, 18,
26, 32). These two events show that, with Jesus' death,
salvation has entered its worldwide dimension.

STUDY QUESTION: As the story of Jesus' death was
handed on, more and more miracu-
lous events were introduced, a process begun already in Matthew
27:51–53. Why would that occur?

15:40–47
Jesus is laid in a tomb

40 There were some women watching from a distance. Among them were Mary of Magdala, Mary
who was the mother of James the younger and
41 Joset, and Salome. ·These used to follow him and
look after him when he was in Galilee. And there
were many other women there who had come up
to Jerusalem with him.
42 It was now evening, and since it was Prepara-
43 tion Day (that is, the vigil of the sabbath), ·there
came Joseph of Arimathaea, a prominent member
of the Council, who himself lived in the hope of
seeing the kingdom of God, and he boldly went to
44 Pilate and asked for the body of Jesus. ·Pilate,
astonished that he should have died so soon, summoned the centurion and inquired if he was al-
45 ready dead. ·Having been assured of this by the
46 centurion, he granted the corpse to Joseph, ·who
bought a shroud, took Jesus down from the cross,
wrapped him in the shroud and laid him in a tomb
which had been hewn out of the rock. He then
rolled a stone against the entrance to the tomb.
47 Mary of Magdala and Mary the mother of Joset
were watching and took note of where he was laid.

☩

Mark's familiar stylistic device of bracketing one tradition with another is again clear in these verses, where
references to the women bracket the account of Jesus'
burial. Their importance as witnesses to Jesus' burial is

thus underscored, and points to the prominence en-
joyed by women in the primitive church, contrary to
their lower status in Jewish culture. Although the sons
of the second Mary mentioned in verse 40 bear the
same names as two of the brothers of Jesus (cf. 6:3),
they were common men's names, and it is difficult to
imagine that Mark would have identified Jesus' mother
in such an ambiguous fashion. Contrary to the account
in John (19:26), neither disciple nor relative was present in Mark's account of Jesus' death. This is the first
time Mark mentions Mary of Magdala, although there
is further information about her in Luke (8:1–3). Such
additional information about prominent persons is typical of the developing tradition.

It was Jewish custom to bury the dead before sunset
(cf. Dt 21:22–23), and responsibility for the burial
was often undertaken by pious Jews of some means
when a person died unattended. Joseph of Arimathaea,
who saw to Jesus' burial, was probably not a follower
of Jesus but rather a pious Jew who, like others (i.e.,
Pharisees, Essenes, Zealots), awaited God's promised
reign on earth. His boldness in requesting the body
shows the request was a favor, but also provides opportunity for the reader to learn that Jesus was in fact
dead (verses 43–45). His resurrection could therefore
not have been merely his revival from the shock of
crucifixion. He had died, and his corpse was laid in a
tomb. That the embalming was postponed is explained
by the fact that the Sabbath was at hand (verse 42).
Such activity could not be undertaken until the Sabbath
had passed (cf. 16:1).

The absence of people who later became prominent
in Christian circles gives this account the flavor of his-

torical remembrance. In some such way Jesus, deserted by his closest followers, must have received burial.

STUDY QUESTION: In what other accounts in Mark do women play a prominent role?

Mark 16:1–8
ON THE THIRD DAY

¹ **16** When the sabbath was over, Mary of Magdala, Mary the mother of James, and Salome, bought spices with which to go and anoint
² him. ·And very early in the morning on the first day of the week they went to the tomb, just as the sun was rising.
³ They had been saying to one another, "Who will roll away the stone for us from the entrance to
⁴ the tomb?" ·But when they looked they could see that the stone—which was very big—had already
⁵ been rolled back. ·On entering the tomb they saw a young man in a white robe seated on the right-hand side, and they were struck with amazement.
⁶ But he said to them, "There is no need for alarm. You are looking for Jesus of Nazareth, who was crucified: he has risen, he is not here. See, here is
⁷ the place where they laid him. ·But you must go and tell his disciples and Peter, 'He is going before you to Galilee; it is there you will see him, just as
⁸ he told you.' " ·And the women came out and ran away from the tomb because they were frightened out of their wits; and they said nothing to a soul, for they were afraid. . . .

✠

Once again, it was the women who attended to Jesus' needs (cf. 15:41). There is a problem in the way they are named, however. If it were not for 15:40, we would read 15:47 as "Mary, the *daughter* of Joses," and 16:1 as "Mary, the *daughter* of James." Perhaps 15:42–47 and 16:1–8 were originally independent traditions, which Mark put together. He then created a continuity between them by means of 15:40, in which those two Marys were assumed to be the same person.

The only name that is consistent in those traditions is "Mary Magdalene." That may be more than coincidental. In this earliest account of the empty tomb, it is only women who see it, yet in the Judaism of that day, a woman could not serve in any legal proceeding as a witness. If one had wanted to create a story which, by citing witnesses that the tomb was empty, would have proved that Jesus had risen from the dead, this would not have been the way to go about it (Lk 24:24 and Jn 20:3–10 later remedy that by having disciples verify that it was empty). Thus the present story may well rest on the historical remembrance that it was Mary Magdalene who first discovered that the tomb was empty (cf. Jn 20:1).

The reaction of the women (verse 8) further shows that Mark did not think the empty tomb gave rise to a joyous Easter faith, or even underlay Christian proclamation. It is clear that Mark knew the resurrection was the key to the meaning of Jesus' whole career (cf. 8:31; 9:9, 31; 10:34). The "young man" in the white robe (verse 5), certainly a divine messenger (verses 6–7), makes it clear God has now raised Jesus from the dead. Why then this story, in which disobedience and fear still dog the risen Jesus as they did the earthly Jesus?

Perhaps Mark wanted to tell us that the momentous events which began with John the Baptist and the ap-

pearance of Jesus (cf. 1:1–9), and which had continued through the public activity of Jesus, did not come
to an end with Jesus' death, or even with his resurrection. Perhaps Mark wanted his readers to understand that what had begun with Jesus was still going
on. Jesus, now risen, continued to lead his disciples
(verse 7) as once he led them to Jerusalem before his
death (10:32). If those events were continuing, then
suffering, ambiguity, and rejection continue as possi-
bilities for those who follow him (cf. 4:14–19). Only
at the last will the harvest come (4:8); only at the last
will Jesus return to gather up his own (13:26–27).
Until then, Jesus' followers must watch and wait
(13:37), knowing their victorious Lord continues to
lead them.

STUDY QUESTION: Does this account in any way prove
                that Jesus rose from the dead?

Mark 16:9–20
EPILOGUE:
DEATH COULD NOT HOLD HIM

⁹ Having risen in the morning on the first day of the week, he appeared first to Mary of Magdala ¹⁰ from whom he had cast out seven devils. ·She then went to those who had been his companions, and who were mourning and in tears, and told them. ¹¹ But they did not believe her when they heard her say that he was alive and that she had seen him. ¹² After this, he showed himself under another form to two of them as they were on their way into ¹³ the country. ·These went back and told the others, who did not believe them either. ¹⁴ Lastly, he showed himself to the Eleven themselves while they were at table. He reproached them for their incredulity and obstinacy, because they had refused to believe those who had seen ¹⁵ him after he had risen. ·And he said to them, "Go out to the whole world; proclaim the Good News ¹⁶ to all creation. ·He who believes and is baptized will be saved; he who does not believe will be con- ¹⁷ demned. ·These are the signs that will be associated with believers: in my name they will cast ¹⁸ out devils; they will have the gift of tongues; ·they will pick up snakes in their hands, and be unharmed should they drink deadly poison; they will lay their hands on the sick, who will recover." ¹⁹ And so the Lord Jesus, after he had spoken to them, was taken up into heaven: there at the right ²⁰ hand of God he took his place, ·while they, going

out, preached everywhere, the Lord working with
them and confirming the word by the signs that
accompanied it.

✠

There are several reasons for thinking these verses
were not written by the person who wrote the rest of
Mark's Gospel. The language is unlike that of the preceding chapters, the passage is absent from some of the
best and oldest manuscripts of Mark, and both Jerome
and Eusebius, two eminent scholars in the early church,
say it was not in their best copies of the New Testament. The passage fits awkwardly into its present context (Mary Magdalene is introduced as though 16:1
were unknown, and 16:3–8 are simply ignored) and
presumes information drawn from the other, later Gospels. It is an amalgam of appearances of Jesus, drawn
from other Gospel accounts, and other traditions. Perhaps it was originally composed as a summary of the
appearances and ascension of the risen Jesus. At some
later point, after both Mark and this passage had been
written, someone decided this material could be used to
supply the lack of appearance stories in Mark.

The information about Mary Magdalene's earlier history (verse 9) is drawn from Luke 8:1–3, and her
meeting with Jesus reflects John 20:14–18. Her report
to the disciples (verse 10) reflects John 20:18, and
their disbelief (verse 11) reflects Luke 24:11. That
Jesus appeared to two followers "under another form"
(verse 12) explains why, in Luke 24:16, they could
not recognize him (cf. Lk 24:13–32). Their report to
the other disciples (verse 13) is also told in Luke

24:33, though the attendant disbelief is not. That unbelief, as verse 14 shows, was a point the author of these verses wanted to emphasize. Jesus' appearance to the assembled disciples (verse 14) reflects Luke 24:36–38 (cf. Jn 20:19; 1 Co 15:5), while the detail that they were at table is also reflected in Acts 10:41.

In addition to chiding disbelief in reports that Jesus had risen from the dead, our author wants to show that the outcome of the resurrection is the universal mission of the church. That is clear from verses 15–20, where again, he draws on other New Testament material. The mission charge (verse 15) is reminiscent of Matthew 28:19 (cf. Ac 1:8), and the resulting division between those who accept the proclamation and those who do not (verse 16) may reflect John 20:23 (cf. Mt 18:18). The accompanying miraculous signs (verses 17–18), except for immunity from poison, are known in the New Testament (devils, Mt 10:1 and Mk 6:7; tongues, Ac 2:4 and 1 Co 12:10 and 14:8; snakes, Ac 28:3–6 and Lk 10:19; healing, Mk 6:13 and Ac 3:1–7 and 14:8–10). Such a story of immunity is told later of one Justus Barsabas, who was said to be the disciple not chosen in Acts 1:23 (so Eusebius, *Church History*, III, 39, 9). Jesus' ascension (Ac 1:9) and his sitting at God's right hand (Ac 7:55; Mk 14:62) are also known in the New Testament, as are the wondrous signs that accompanied the apostles' preaching (Ac 2:43; 5:12; 6:8; 8:6; 15:12).

If these verses are not Markan, they are in the canon, and we can profit from their point. Witness to Jesus, risen from the dead and now with God, remains the unique task of the church, and if, like those earliest followers, we do not always accept or perform as we ought, the risen Christ continues to challenge us to fulfill the task he entrusted to his followers.

STUDY QUESTION: What do you think is the most important point these verses want to make?

SUGGESTED FURTHER READINGS

Achtemeier, Paul J. *Mark*. Proclamation Commentaries. Philadelphia: Fortress, 1975. Paper. Discussion of the theological motifs and emphases of the Gospel, intended to supplement commentaries on Mark.

Anderson, Hugh. *The Gospel of Mark*. Century Bible. London: Oliphants, 1976. A readable, authoritative commentary on Mark, in traditional commentary form.

Hargreaves, John. *A Guide to St. Mark's Gospel*. TEF Study Guide 2. Naperville, Ill.: Alec R. Allenson, 1965. Paper. An introduction to the Gospel, in simplified language, with numerous study suggestions.

Linden, Philip Van. *Gospel of St. Mark*. Read and Pray. Chicago: Franciscan Herald, 1976. Paper. Brief observations, reflections seek out the theological and devotional import of the Gospel. Short prayers invite the reader to pray the gospel.

McCarter, Neely. *Help Me Understand, Lord*. Philadelphia: Westminster Press, 1978. Prayer responses to the message of Mark's Gospel.

Nineham, D. E. *St. Mark*. Pelican Gospel Commentaries. Baltimore: Penguin Books, 1963. Paper. Passage-by-passage study, with good notes on the social and cultural conditions of Mark's time.

Perrin, Norman. *What Is Redaction Criticism?* Guides

to Biblical Scholarship. Philadelphia: Fortress, 1969. Paper. A good introduction to the method now widely used in studying the Gospels, with examples of how it operates.

Schenke, Ludger. *Glory and the Way of the Cross: The Gospel of Mark*. Tr. R. Scroggs. Herald Biblical Booklets. Chicago: Franciscan Herald, 1972. Paper. A brief introduction to some of the theological and literary problems in Mark.

Schweizer, Eduard. *The Good News According to Mark*. Tr. D. H. Madvig. Atlanta: John Knox Press, 1970. Perhaps the most authoritative commentary on the Gospel of Mark now available in English, it combines solid scholarship with a vibrant faith.

OTHER IMAGE BOOKS

OTHER IMAGE BOOKS

OTHER IMAGE BOOKS

OTHER IMAGE BOOKS